D1442849

Literacy and the
Survival of Humanism

Literacy and the Survival of Humanism

Richard A. Lanham

Yale University Press   New Haven and London

Designed by Nancy Ovedovitz and set in VIP Meridian type. Printed in the United States of America by Edwards Brothers Inc., Ann Arbor, Michigan.

Library of Congress Cataloging in Publication Data

Lanham, Richard A.
  Literacy and the survival of humanism.
  Includes index.
  1. English philology—Study and teaching.
2. Education, Humanistic. 3. Humanism. 4. Rhetoric—Study and teaching. 5. Literature—Study and teaching.
I. Title.
PE65.L33 1983   808'.042   83-3618
ISBN 0-300-02968-3
ISBN 0-300-02985-3 (paper)

10   9   8   7   6   5   4   3   2   1

For William David Schaefer

Contents

Preface

It is not so new as we might think, this attempt to keep the teaching of literature and the teaching of composition in some kind of humane relationship with each other. The first professor of English ever appointed—the Reverend Thomas Dale, who began his duties at University College, London, in 1828—found himself more concerned with language than with literature: "He lectured three times a week to a regular class on the principles of composition."* And the attempt to tell students how both literature and composition relate to the larger welfare of society seems just as venerable. The historian just quoted tells us of a master at Eton in the 1840s remonstrating with an idle schoolboy in this way:

> If you do not take more pains, how can you ever expect to write good longs and shorts? If you do not write good longs and shorts, how can you ever be a man of taste? If you are not a man of taste, how can you ever be of use in the world? [p. 12]

It is Latin composition that vexed the professor here, and not English, but the hunger revealed is the same. We must somehow get from verbal patterns to taste, and from taste to politics; from composition to literature, and from literature to "use in the world." And if we are to laugh at the simplicity of this Etonic progression, we should do so with a knowledge that our own may depend as much on custom, and as little on logic, as this mid-nineteenth-century triple equation.

The essays in this volume try to sketch out the same three-stage movement from composition to literature to "use in the world." In their original versions they were not written with an eye to sequential reading, but perhaps that makes them more relevant for the subject in hand, the endeavor to hold different kinds of inquiry together, to see how they work in the world and, in the case of the last essay, to put them to work in that world. The essays were written during a period when I was trying, in my own mind and career, to balance literature, composition, and the administrative duties that a major curricular reform required. It might help the reader if I tried, here

*D. J. Palmer, *The Rise of English Studies* (London, 1965), p. 21.

at the beginning, to explain why these disparate undertakings seem
to me a single endeavor.

The Greek rhetoricians, in their search for what persuades man,
created a theory of motivation firmly based on the evolutionary nature
of Homo sapiens. What that nature is, we are right now finding out
by inquiry pursued in the several different areas of evolutionary
behavioral biology, inquiry that is giving us, at long last, what Plato's
Socrates accused rhetoric of lacking—a *technē*, a general theory of
human motivation and behavior, a central body of knowledge. This
theory, an interdisciplinary expansion of the Post-Darwinian synthesis,
has not yet been formulated in a great philosophical document, but
it has emerged in many fields: social anthropology, perceptual psychology, ethnology, sociobiology, game theory, among others. It re-
states, in empirical terms, the doctrine of Original Sin, returning to
us a human nature by no means always trailing clouds of glory. This
return has distressed many people today, just as it distressed Plato.
Plato's formulation of the problem has, alas, governed the subsequent
debate, and an imaginative presentation of the rhetorician's view of
man has been hard to come by. As a result, the Western rhetorical
tradition has tried to discuss and develop rhetorical theory in a Platonic
universe which contradicts rhetoric at every point. Aristotle's *Rhetoric*
provides the first great instance of this continual and methodical self-
contradiction, but almost every great rhetorical text since has done
the same thing. And the freshman composition texts repeat the error.

The following essays argue that the Post-Darwinian synthesis, by
giving us a new way to think about human behavior, also gives us
a new way to think about rhetoric, about literature, and about their
relationship, as that works itself out in the university curriculum.
These three worlds—composition, literature, and humanist curriculum—are being revitalized by the same evolutionary theory of behavior,
and that revolution provides, finally, the central means of relating
them.

Versions of six of these essays have been read at professional meetings:
"Aristotle and the Illusion of Purpose," at the 1979 Conference on
College Composition and Communication; "The Choice of Utopias:
More or Castiglione?" at the Symposium on Thomas More sponsored

by the UCLA Center for Medieval and Renaissance Studies in 1978;*
"*At* and *Through*: The Opaque Style and Its Uses," at the Tudor and
Stuart Club of The Johns Hopkins University, 1980; "The Chaucerian
Biogrammar and the Takeover of Culture," at the English Institute,
Harvard University, 1978; "Post-Darwinian Humanism," at the Sym-
posium on Rhetoric of the North Texas Area Universities, 1979 (pub-
lished in *The State of the Profession*, a special number of the *ADE
Bulletin*, Fall 1979); "Should English Departments Take an Interest
in Teaching Composition?" at the 1981 convention of the Modern
Language Association of America (published in *Literature and Composition: Bridging the Gap*, ed. W. Horner, University of Chicago Press,
1982). "The Abusage of Usage" appeared in the *Virginia Quarterly
Review* (Winter 1977).

For their inspiration and affection during the period when I wrote
these essays I must thank my colleagues who began the UCLA Writing
Programs with me: Carol P. Hartzog, Susan L. Fletcher, Patricia S.
Taylor, Ruth Mitchell, Robin Jeffers, Julie Bisceglia, and Mike Rose.
I also owe a real and continuing debt of gratitude to Lauren Cammack
and Susan Bukowski for the kind of intelligent and imaginative staff
support that academics dream about but seldom find.

From the beginning of the Writing Programs, one of our staunchest
friends was the Vice-Chancellor of Instructional Development, Andrea
Rich. Without her help and encouragement we would never have
got off the ground; without her sparkling realism the flight would
not have been nearly so much fun.

In trying to find my way around in behavioral biology, I have been
very lucky to have as friend and colleague Robert Jay Russell of the
UCLA Department of Anthropology. By putting my hypotheses, especially those that touch on sociobiology, under the keenest pressure,
he has helped me orient my thinking in a cluster of fields which are
changing with bewildering rapidity.

My greatest obligation during this period, however, is owed to my
friend Bill Schaefer, the Executive Vice-Chancellor at UCLA. He has

* Later published as a chapter in Mary J. Carruthers and Elizabeth D. Kirk,
eds., *Acts of Interpretation: The Text in Its Context* (Norman, Okla.: Pilgrim Books,
1982).

shown throughout his career how the humanist can serve the cause of goodness in the world, and never more than in the years when I was privileged to have him as my boss and, in watching him work, came to see what "grace under pressure" was really all about.

Ellen Graham of Yale University Press has edited the manuscript of this book, and evidence of her editorial skill and scholarly good judgment can be found in every chapter, indeed on almost every page. This is the second Yale book we have done together and it is a wonderful comradeship. I was lucky enough to work with another old Yale Press friend too, Barbara Folsom, and her editing has spared the reader much vexation of spirit.

Chapter 1
Introduction

It may be that the gulfs will wash us down:
It may be we shall touch the Happy Isles,
And see the great Achilles, whom we knew.
—Tennyson, "Ulysses"

Gulfs seem to threaten us everywhere we turn nowadays in English studies—gulfs between the various chronological fields of English study, between English literary study and English composition, between graduate training in English and the teaching assignments that follow it, between classical rhetoric and modern composition, above all between traditional rhetoric and the inquiries into "rhetorical" behavior going forward in fields from mathematics to primatology, from perception psychology to cell biology. In the several years that I have been reading in some of these fields, I have often marveled at their isolation from one another. It was almost like journeying between hermetically sealed capsules of thought.

The most obvious gulf I encountered was that between literary study and composition. For half a dozen years I had been working in Renaissance literature and in composition, and the two areas seemed to me so alike that moving from one to the other was easy and indeed almost inevitable. We had to do with two literacy crises, two media crises (first into and then out of the Gutenberg era), two revolutions in the university curriculum—above all, two lightning flashes of self-consciousness, vertiginous glimpses into the grounds of human motive. To study the educational struggles of the Oxford Reformers or Castiglione's effort to make political, social, and curricular sense of style or More's plea in *Utopia* to outlaw it or Shakespeare's dramatic meditations on dramatic motives or Rabelais's rhetorical cartoons of humanistic thinking drawn in upon itself—to reflect on all these was to study a literacy crisis very like our own.

Thus it seemed natural enough that someone who had been ruminating these issues might try his own hand at an educational experiment, an effort at reforming the rhetorical curriculum, as I did when we began the UCLA Writing Programs in July 1979. To do something like this was, albeit in a humble way, simply to imitate

1

Colet, Castiglione, Mulcaster, Ramus, even—who knows?—John Milton. Our contemporary perils are more unnerving than those of the Renaissance; we are apt to think far more in metaphors of death than of rebirth. And our new world-consciousness, though it may sparkle intermittently with the excitement of exploring space or eliminating smallpox, is finally doom-laden, suffused with despair. But the similarities remain striking. It seemed natural, since I had pondered the earlier literacy crisis for a dozen years, to lend a hand at coping with our present one. Never, clearly, had the need been so great.

My friends did not think so. Nor did that small part of the learned world in which I was privileged to dwell. They all thought I was crazy. I was deserting "The Renaissance" for "Composition." It was as if a moderately well-established orthopedic surgeon had decided to abandon his practice and open an inner-city clinic in chiropractic acupuncture. The gulf I had encountered was not only an intellectual one, it was social and economic as well. The world of composition was the helot stratum in literary study; it was the great Cave of Boredom and Despair from which you escaped, usually by painful stages, to the Sunny Uplands of the Graduate Seminar. The world of composition was pedagogy-centered and application-oriented. It supplied, such as they were, the engineering applications of literary study. Its social and intellectual energies flowed upward from the schools and not downward from the discipline and its national organization. My literary colleagues thought of this world only to despise it. Part of this feeling was the scornful dismissal of the secondary-school world, and especially of teacher training, which has characterized research-oriented literature departments since the end of World War II. Part of it, too, was the rejection of any "service function" for a literature department, a rejection that extended also to giving courses in humanities or general studies.

This contempt was reciprocated from the other side. The world of composition had its own journals, meetings, professional associations, old-person network (it has had far more women in it from the beginning than the literary world)—in fact, a whole separate career game. When I attended my first meeting in this world, I thought I might escape safely if I read a paper on Aristotle ("Aristotle and the Illusion of Purpose"), an author canonical enough to keep me out of trouble. Not so. The keynote speaker for the convention singled out and denounced "literati," like me, who were invading the composition establishment from the literary world. There has been a mad kind of hatred between the two worlds, and I have discussed its bizarre pathology and malign effects in several chapters of this book. As I have tried to show in "*At* and *Through*," as well as in "The Abusage of Usage" and "Post-Darwinian Humanism," the two worlds are separated by different theories of language. But more than this, they seem separated by the gulf between theory and practice. Any attempt to put the two together rings an alarm bell. I had included, for example, in the More and Castiglione essay ("The Choice of Utopias") a short discussion of the implications of their fundamental disagreement for the modern composition curriculum. We were, I felt, fighting the same battle all over right now, and this seemed worthy of remark. But the organizer of the conference, a Renaissance scholar, insisted that this section be removed. It was not "germane to the conference." The only interest that literary people feel obliged to take in the literacy crisis is to play what in "The Abusage of Usage" I call "Fowler games," to go off in a collective snit at changing patterns in English usage.

This settled disciplinary scorn is more than just a routine example of academic bitchery. It is part of a larger estrangement, one that has been intensifying for the last thirty years. The disciplinary focus of the college and university curriculum has become so narrow that it has tried to filter everything else out, to purify the university into an institute for advanced study, a research and graduate training institute. The composition world was the logical focus for this general repudiation of impure elements. The University of California provides, I think, the extreme case in American academic life, and so perhaps I can use it as an example. When I joined the UCLA faculty in 1965, the campus was transported by an exalting rumor: the university system was about to get rid of lower-division instruction altogether, give it to the state colleges and offer only upper-division and graduate training—concentrate entirely, that is, on instruction as organized by departmental and professional discipline. This was thought to be—and is still thought to be—the quintessential university structure, the university as in itself it ought to be. And, for English studies, composition came to represent everything that this vision excluded: remediation, the ordinary tedious training in how to write scholarly prose, general education, the whole nondisciplinary focus of the first two under-graduate years, teacher training, and interest in the secondary-school curriculum.

After I had been washed down into this gulf between composition and literary study I began to ponder the fall-guy role for composition. Could something positive be made of it? Was composition the natural synecdoche for the neglected areas in the university curriculum? Wasn't this in fact what I had been arguing all along? If so, maybe something could be made of the pariah; around composition could cluster a revival of the nondisciplinary first two years, the much lamented general-education part of the university curriculum. As I argued in "Post-Darwinian Humanism," the crucial area for any curricular reconstruction would be the first two years. From them everything flowed. The standards they required would determine the level of accomplishment required in the schools. And if the first two years gave the students no real general education, the specialized disciplinary and departmentalized education of the second two years would be premature specialization. It could not honestly proceed. Either it would become an ignorant specialization, built around a hollow core, or it would suspend the specialization to build the core first, thereby denying the orderly sequence it seemed to argue for. Failure of sequence was the endemic illness of the whole American educational system from beginning to end. The restoration of sequence had to begin now and it had to begin somewhere. The logical starting point seemed to me the first two undergraduate years. The problem here was that no one knew what to do with these first two years. The old notion of a liberal education had finally collapsed and nobody knew what to put in its place.

I thought that I knew. Or, rather, that I could restate a strand of the traditional Renaissance argument in such a way as to make it both comprehensible and alive. The issue could be nicely posed by comparing two Renaissance utopias, Sir Thomas More's in *Utopia* and Baldassare Castiglione's in *The Courtier*. Every utopia is a curriculum and vice versa—that is why curricular debate never ends. These two fundamentally opposed utopias were the basic types. If we saw them clearly, I argued in "The Choice of Utopias," we would also see the basic curricular choice clearly as one between theories of motive. This is just the choice that underlies the theoretical confusion about composition. In "Aristotle and the Illusion of Purpose" and in "The Abusage of Usage," I have explored this confusion, and in "*At* and *Through*" I have tried to schematize it in a theoretical way. This last essay tries to bring the root stylistic misunderstanding about the role of self-consciousness into some contact with the basic arguments of literary criticism, and of the visual arts as well. Understanding the role of self-consciousness in verbal style, I argued, would lead to a theory of motive that could stimulate a genuinely new way of comparing the arts to one another. And that was one way to construct a new interdisciplinary humanistic curriculum.

When, in "Post-Darwinian Humanism," I brought together these three concerns—composition, curriculum, humanism—I thereby fell into the yet deeper gulf between the humanities and evolutionary biology. I had begun to read in this area long before sociobiology made the cover of *Time* magazine;* and subsequently, with the aid of Jay Russell, a primatologist at UCLA, I had begun to educate myself in the genetic and other issues involved in the sociology debate. The relevance of this line of inquiry, of the whole Post-Darwinian synthesis, to rhetoric seemed to me both so immediate and so clear that I started to integrate it into my thinking and writing. I got into trouble every time I did so. It set off land mines in ways that I found both bewildering and utterly surprising: I was a dupe of genetic determinism (a colleague's comment on "Post-Darwinian Humanism"); I was a disciple of that well-known fascist biologist Konrad Lorenz (a comment from the audience at the English Institute, after I had read "The Chaucerian Biogrammar and the Takeover of Culture"); I was guilty of "an uncritical endorsement of sociobiology" (a reader of the manuscript for this book in an earlier version). And so on.

---

* For me, the basic works were: Niko Tinbergen, *The Herring Gull's World* (New York, 1961; 1967); Lionel Tiger and Robin Fox, *The Imperial Animal* (New York, 1971); Edward O. Wilson, *Sociobiology* (Cambridge, Mass., 1975); Richard Dawkins, *The Selfish Gene* (New York, 1976); D. P. Barash, *Sociobiology and Behavior* (New York, 1977); and Richard D. Alexander's provocative series of articles, later summarized in *Darwinism and Human Affairs* (Seattle and London, 1979).

The moral seemed clear. Don't do in practice what everyone appears to recommend doing in principle; don't try to heal the split between the two cultures; nobody in any field really wants this kind of cross-disciplinary work to be done. In my own case, moreover, I had strayed into what became the sociobiology battleground without even knowing that it was to become a battleground and without sufficiently qualifying and explaining.

Given a fresh chance, I submit an explanation. Ever since I had begun to study classical rhetoric I had been interested in the Greek Sophists. I had concluded that there must be more to them and their arguments than Plato's nasty caricatures reveal; then I came across H. I. Marrou's surprisingly sympathetic description of them in *A History of Education in Antiquity*. Marrou had, to be sure, a guilty conscience and kept apologizing for qualifying the Platonic abuse that had lasted from Plato to Werner Jaeger, but he tried to make sense of what the Sophists were doing by asking the fundamental questions: if they were as silly as Plato made them out to be, why were they so popular? why did the rhetorical curriculum last so long? why did it triumph over the philosophical one? and why did it become the fundamental Western *paideia*? W. K. C. Guthrie had asked the same questions, I learned; and in a different way so had Mario Untersteiner, in his study of the Sophists. And then I read two books that constituted an epiphany for me: Eric Havelock's *A Preface to Plato* and *The Liberal Temper in Greek Politics*. In *The Liberal Temper* especially, Havelock tried to reconstruct the whole intellectual and educational position out of which the Sophists, and indeed Greek rhetoric as a whole, had developed. I had been thinking on just these lines, and here was a world-famous Hellenist developing the argument I could only guess at.

That rhetorical world view which Havelock developed answered the resonant question that Plato's Socrates had posed for the whole of Western education and thought: what was the *technē* of rhetoric? what was its natural subject matter? what did it study that philosophy did not? The answer returned, in its simplest form, was this: rhetoric accepted two areas of human motive which Platonic philosophy did not—game and play. Game meant the whole area of ludic struggle, of invidious comparison, of status-seeking, of everything that Christianity was to call pride. Play meant the spontaneous need to engage in certain attitudes whether they were elicited by pressing circumstance or not. Play was nonpurposive motive, and since it lay outside the domain of rational (i.e., purposive) explanation, it was potentially subversive. Rhetoric accepted these two ranges of motive and tried to integrate them with ordinary practical purpose; philosophy deplored these motives and tried to banish them. This was exactly the basic contrast between Castiglione's *Courtier* and More's *Utopia*. And it was the basic argument in composition theory, that between the reigning orthodoxy, which chose to banish style, and the remnant of the rhetorical tradition, which defended it—a remnant I had tried to resurrect in *Style: An Anti-Textbook* (1974). And it was the crucial issue in how you defined humanism. The confusion about whether to include play and game or to leave them out of human motive had been from the beginning the essential internal self-contradiction of the humanist tradition. I had tried to make this point, apropos a series of Renaissance texts, in *The Motives of Eloquence* (1976).

And now along came the Post-Darwinian synthesis—more especially what, until it became a nasty word, was called sociobiology. It argued that if we consider Homo sapiens as a primate in his evolutionary framework, we must first of all see that he comes upon the scene with a lot of evolutionary baggage, a lot of behavior patterns that are programmed to happen, a lot of things that he just "wants to do" because that is part of his nature. Man has a "human nature" after all, and a central element in that nature, that "primate bio-grammar" as Tiger and Fox called it, is status seeking. Primates are status animals. Their society is based on it. Emulous striving is at the heart of the leftover evolutionary baggage. People, then, like to play at all kinds of things, but especially they like to compete. They like games. And there it was—the *technē* of Rhetoric, the range of motive to which Sophists pointed as fundamental to man's nature, the reason why the rhetorical curriculum lasted so long. Rhetoric, then, had a proper theory of motive at last, and this theory was grounded in man's evolutionary nature, in the kind of primate that he is. Rhetoric was, had been all along, a genuinely *evolutionary* theory of style—in the last analysis, a theory of behavior. To see this clearly was, it seemed to me, to "recover the classical past" for real, to carry forward what the Renaissance had begun.

For my purposes, it did not really matter whether sociobiology could sustain its case in an extreme form or not. I did not care, finally, *how* hard-wired human behavior really was. That would be left to the geneticists in any event. Almost no one, in the long run, would support the extreme culturalist point of view that Homo sapiens enters the world as a tabula rasa, that man has no nature, only nurture. And at what point the nature/nurture argument balanced out was really, from the rhetorical point of view, irrelevant. The vital issue was that human nature is and always will be a battleground between play, game, and purpose. That the balances struck will always change and shift seems to be so obvious as to go without saying. We shall always have "free will." (Indeed, if recent work with such things as hitchhiking alleles and jumping genes is anything to go by, we may have more chance in the living universe than we know what to do with.) The relation between genetic and cultural evolution runs just along this fault line. And, given the plate tectonics of our evolutionary nature, there will always be movement along the fault.

What evolutionary biology offered to the kinds of problems I was trying to solve was a historical and biological explanation for the tripartite theory of motive I had already observed in other areas.

In *composition:* the rhetorical tradition, though seldom recognizing it, was just this combination of play, game, and purpose. It was just this full tradition, now clearly understood and biologically based, which would form the basis of a genuinely New Rhetoric.

In *literature:* the spheres of game and play, not simply of motiveless malignity but of motiveless motive of all sorts, seemed now to be just the particular subject of literature and to constitute its "literariness." The "Chaucerian biogrammar" was finally the fundamental literary biogrammar.

In *humanism:* modern accounts of the humanist curriculum, of the liberal essence of liberal learning, fell neatly into three groups: one ("Progressivism") maximized play and banished game and purpose; the second (the nineteenth-century "playing fields of Eton" school) maximized game and banished pure play and purpose; and the proponents of training, technical or vocational, avowed purpose and abjured play and game.

Only a few modern theorists—Whitehead prominent among them— argued against this ritual purification of motive and recommended an impurity, a dynamic mixture of three motives. But with their aid we could begin to see the behavioral center of the humanities—the effort to bring the three conflicting ranges of human motive into some kind of balance. The great Western literary texts tried to do this directly, but *any* text or inquiry could do it too. Humanism was a characteristic attitude and endeavor, not a list of canonical texts.

One need not be duped by sociobiology into a premature genetic determinism in order to see how radically important evolutionary biology was for these three areas of inquiry. It showed how they were related. And, in doing so, it showed how the humanities and the biological part of the sciences, at least, can get together in an essentially integrated curriculum. We can simply put aside all the stale clichés about the humanities; we can see the kernel of truth lurking in the dead, though recently resuscitated, "core" curricula and build upon this kernel. We can design a humanistic curriculum from the inside out, as a training in self-conscious motive, and not, as with a list of set texts that "guarantee" liberation, from the outside in.

But how, in practice, does one do this? The "in practice" was essential. The rhetorical tradition, whether in classical Greece or Renaissance England, was a program for action, not a theoretical exercise. I address the question in the last three essays in this book but can give no full answer to it: the experiment is still in progress, has in fact barely begun. Nevertheless, it has been a genuine "learning experience," as the psychologists say, and some of the lessons learned may be useful for others contemplating similar endeavors. For there have been several new gulfs to fall into here too.

How to begin? The answer here was easy. If, as I argue in "Should English Departments Take an Interest in Teaching Composition?", our outstanding problems in the humanities curriculum all led to composition, it was equally clear that composition was the only practical starting point. To try to begin an experimental program in the humanities—especially one like this, based on a revolutionary reappraisal of man—would have involved endless talk. But the need for composition was manifest and generally acknowledged. We would begin there. It was to the literacy crisis in its widest sense that a really new humanism would have to address itself anyway. A radical theory needed, at least at first, a conservative practice.

I had no problem with this seeming self-contradiction. The Clarity-Brevity-Sincerity, or C-B-S, theory of composition that we would start with was true for part of the domain of style. I had written the *Revising Prose* textbooks in this narrow subset of a general theory of style and knew its uses. And I knew that it fit into the larger domain I had sketched out in *Style: An Anti-Textbook*, provided only that we knew *where* it fit. It failed only when it masqueraded as a general theory; as *part* of a general theory, it would always have its important uses. So we would begin with a broad service program in composition, the UCLA Writing Programs, and see where it led, or could be made to lead. It would begin with pressing problems, with Whitehead's "insistent present," and we would see what emerged.

What emerged were more gulfs. The first was a fundamental gap between the administration and the faculty. I don't mean here the usual sharpshooting between the two but a deeper division, and one that I am convinced occurs even in cozier academic contexts than the vast University of California. In the administration of UC there was no commonly shared educational philosophy. It was this central vacuum that Clark Kerr elevated into a principle when he called the university a series of diverse interests united by a common parking problem. The joke, it turned out, was an old one (the common bond used to be a heating plant), and it illustrated nicely Lawrence Veysey's thesis that the only common focus the twentieth-century American university had was a bureaucratic one. At UCLA the pressures of the 1960s had distilled this administrative principle-of-diffuse-purposes into pure crisis-management. You simply responded to the outside pressures as they occurred, with fixes quick and not so quick. These fixes did not fall into any pattern, make any corporate sense, *go anywhere.* They were just stacked atop one another. Basic skills programs, tutorials, learning labs, counseling programs for the under-prepared students; a new honors program because the bright white middle-class overachieving students were all going to Yale or Stanford or Berkeley; a new "core" curriculum for the middle of the student sandwich.

All these activities had in common was that the faculty did not really care about them. They were all "service" functions, not properly academic because they fell outside the disciplinary and career-game boundaries which defined acceptable academic reality. There were a whole cluster of these "service" functions lost in academic limbo. Together they constituted just the activities where reconstruction of the lower-division curriculum would begin. They were the essential activities if we were to solve the essential problem—the failure of educational sequence that had come from the dissolution of the first two undergraduate years. *And nobody wanted them.* The faculty, which might be expected to know what to do, wanted no part of them; the administration, which did not know what to do, still had to do something, though—being, remember, a crisis-management team— it hardly knew what. Anyone willing to step into this gulf from the academic side could take over the lot. I started with the central service function—the teaching of writing. When we began the Writing Programs, we all thought we would be awash in bureaucratic obstacles. There were some, but very few. What surprised us was not the difficulty but the eerie ease of establishing this new service. Here was a central function that everyone agreed needed to be performed but that nobody wanted to perform. It was bizarre. In precisely the areas where the university would increasingly have to respond to social pressures, there was no idea of how to respond. *And no workable machinery of response.*

When we started to staff our programs, we came across yet another root anomaly. In our first hiring campaign, we reviewed over three hundred applications. Almost all the candidates were trained as literary specialists. Much the greatest part of their education was in very narrowly defined periods, genres, or special authors. And this specialization was built on no general base. One read back through the transcripts in vain trying to find a general education on which the ultimate graduate specialization could be built. Yet most of the teaching that such people would do was in composition, not literature. It had always been this way—even during the go-go years of the 1960s. And most of the literary teaching would be in general literature and humanities courses, not in specialized seminars. New Ph.D.'s were trained for a world they would never inhabit, a world which—except for a few research universities in the go-go years—had never existed. Trying to find good composition teachers, our immediate problem, was just the extreme case of a general problem. There was a tremendous glut of would-be college professors of English, but they were all trained to be specialists and to scorn other kinds of employment. There was, on the other hand, an enormous need for people trained to teach the courses that had to be offered—courses in writing and the humanities in general. And the graduate programs simply kept stamping out specialists, specialists doomed to be the clerks of a forgotten mood. An administration bemused about what to do with the lower division would get no help from the new faculty, either. A day with the dossiers left you speechless with wonder.

Another gulf: we began to offer a series of writing courses attached to courses in other disciplines. We found that standards of excellence varied alarmingly from department to department and field to field. We had to do not with different styles but almost with different professional languages. Our instructors, speaking only the humanist language, had to do some quick studying. And we had to confront a theoretical problem as well. Was there a common language on campus? Did we have an adequate general theory of prose style? Were we justified in trying to translate sociologese into English? We began to see the campus from the student's point of view: it was a collection of foreign countries called disciplines. No wonder the students wanted to select a major the minute they came on campus. They needed a home to keep from feeling schizoid.

The larger issues posed by the literacy crisis for departments of English, I tried to focus in the essay on English departments and composition. The other specific problems that we faced in beginning a program such as ours at UCLA, I have described in the last essay in the book. Both essays argue that we must put into practice what I have chosen to call Post-Darwinian humanism. Perhaps the reader's progress will be eased if I outline what I mean by this term; in one way or another all the essays try to define it.

Humanism in our time will have to be Castiglione's kind, not More's. It will have to *include* style, not banish it. It must, that is, acknowledge the leftover evolutionary baggage, the impulses of game and play from which style emerges. The central crisis in man's management of his own affairs will be a crisis of self-consciousness rather than a crisis of ethics. We shall have to practice a kind of rhetorical judo on ourselves, learn to discipline, balance, and domesticate the various motives built into us. Just what these are and to what degree they are genetically programmed, we should know fairly soon. We shall no longer be able to practice the ethical solution More recommends, banishing play and game (he calls them Pride) in the name of purpose. In finding their source, we shall have both legitimated all our motives and acknowledged their permanence. The ways to balance these kinds of motives will have to be self-consciously decided upon rather than embraced dogmatically. We shall have to construct our social human nature self-consciously, exactly as Castiglione—and indeed the profoundest thinkers of the Renaissance as a whole—had foreseen. Now that crisis in self-consciousness has come.

Managing people in large numbers has always been an affair of sublime dogmatism, not of self-consciousness. It is Marx and Mao who break down the gates, not Oscar Wilde. Yet this will have to change if we are to develop the kind of homeostatic social regulators which will allow us, with our vast numbers and our lethal new toys, to survive. Bringing this change about is the task of Post-Darwinian humanism. And to succeed, it will have to become an action program. It can no longer afford to brag that, like poetry, it makes nothing happen. In the long struggle between philosophy and rhetoric for the curriculum, rhetoric will have to win again. We shall have to recognize an activity for which I can think of no better name than humanist engineering. We shall have to stop trying to purify our motives and learn to mix them carefully instead. It was just this point which Castiglione sought to make when he invented the paradoxical word *sprezzatura*, the spontaneous affectation that self-consciously chooses to harmonize the various parts of our human nature and then pretends that this harmony is as natural as breathing. And it was just this point, too, that the Sophists were trying to make in constructing the Greek *paideia*. We are dealing here, I take it, with the central generative concept of civility, of sociality itself.

Society, all this is to say, will grow much more self-conscious about how it behaves and why. It will, in fact, come to plot its motives on a matrix very like the one I have suggested in "*At* and *Through*" as the basis for statements about style. This is not accidental. The issue of self-consciousness, and the need for ever-new cybernetically stable resolutions of it, remains the same issue whether it is posed in the domain of style, of the curriculum, or of humanism.

I can suggest, then, that the essays in this volume, though they are argued in all three of these domains, develop the same argument in each. If the argument is true, we possess a body of concepts by which to reach across the gulfs between composition, literature, and the humanities. And if that is so, we can answer the central educational question for the university in our time: What rationale should govern the first two undergraduate years? What is it that we all need to know and share? What common ground do we stand upon? The old humanism, which tried both to repudiate stylistic motive (like More) and to include it (like Castiglione), simply doesn't work anymore. And we need something that works.

Chapter 2
Aristotle and the
Illusion of Purpose

Rhetorical treatises tend to be, more often than we remark, treatises about motive. This makes sense, obviously; any theory of persuasion must finally imply a theory of motive, whether confessedly so or not. Less obviously, though no less essentially, every theory of motive implies a theory of individual identity and social reality. And, *much* less obviously, but with a handy circularity for our purposes, every theory of self and society implies a conception of language and language teaching. I want to sketch out this circle of implications in Aristotle's *Rhetoric.* For the Aristotelian pattern, which has characterized the Western rhetorical tradition ever since Aristotle, represents precisely what will have to change if we are ever to have a genuinely New Rhetoric.

We are treating, in discussions about rhetoric, with two opposed conceptions of language and social reality. Let me describe them, for narrative ease, as two different countries. Just to have convenient neutral names for them, let's call one *Eden* and the other *Post-Darwinia.* In Eden, man is born with a central self, a soul, somewhere in the middle of his head presumably, or his chest. This self is detachable from society in the Stoic way, and society amounts to the sum of these detachable selves and shares their ontological finality. The self does not change when in society. In society or out, it remains the same, *just out there.* And so does the society of such selves, a society *just out there,* too. And so with external physical reality as well. In Eden, the garden is real in the same way Adam and Eve are real, created by God. In this Edenic world, people do things for entirely purposive reasons, eat because they feel hungry, buy a car for transportation, and so on, rather than for competition or stylistic display. Post-Darwinia residents act very differently. Their selves are created, not from the inside out but from the outside in, by a continuing social drama in which, as they learn first one role and then another, they begin to accrete a felt sense of identity. Social reality, in Post-Darwinia, possesses no independent ontological security guaranteed by God. If the social drama stops, reality stops. As a result, your average Post-Darwinian spends a lot of time acting just to keep the social drama revved up, acting for the sake of acting.

The Founding Father of Eden proceeded on what, in the language of modern-day social science, we would call a severely culturalist premise. Edenists were all to be created from scratch, with no past history, their minds a tabula rasa (this last, as Milton shows us, necessitating a good deal of angelic explanation from time to time), and their hearts innocent. They live, thus, in a perpetual present, sail into the world trailing no cloudy propensities to misbehave. Everything they do, they do in response to an external stimulus, suggesting that the Founding Father may have read B. F. Skinner. Far otherwise it stands with the Post-Darwinian folk. No Founding Father sponged their slate clean before sending them into the world. They don't even have a Founding Father, Post-Darwinia having, like Topsy, just growed. They do, however, have a past; and an extremely shady one it is, too. They descend, of course, from an ancient race, but one that had, to borrow a phrase from George Eliot's Mr. Brooke, "gone into a good many things" at one time or another. The Post-Darwinians thus inherit propensities to act in various pronounced ways, given half a chance, especially to compete with one another for dominance and prestige. And, often, they will act without any stimulus at all, in a motival vacuum, just because they are genetically programmed to act that way. They come into the world, then, not nakedly innocent but wearing genes.

Now education, especially education in language, must obviously proceed in very different ways in these two lands. In Eden, language exists to expedite plain purpose and to reflect the independent self accurately. Thus utter transparency is prized there. They teach their children how to speak and write according to the Clarity-Brevity-Sincerity—or, as the Edenists say for short, the C-B-S theory of language. How differently the verbal *paideia* proceeds in Post-Darwinia! Although they acknowledge the virtues of the C-B-S theory, it can account for only a small part of their behavior. In the first place, it assumes a wholly purposive theory of motive, and the Post-Darwinians, as we have just seen, spend a great deal of time in "social reality maintenance" or, as they somewhat vulgarly call it, "just screwing around." And since language forms part of the behavior that keeps the social drama going, briefer is not always better. Nor, since verbal behavior constitutes reality as well as reflecting it, can clarity be a final goal. And Post-Darwinians have trouble writing sincerely, too, since they must first decide which of their selves to be sincere to. Since they form the self by imitating roles, imitation naturally plays a far stronger role in their writing instruction, too—hence all the devices of verbal play.

Altogether, we have here two very different ways to teach language. The Post-Darwinians use the Edenic C-B-S theory, but as part of a larger range of behavior. The Edenists, by contrast, deliberately repudiate Post-Darwinian levity (the Edenists are, it must be said, a solemn lot), calling it Hypocrisy, Pride, Sin.

Which of these motival landscapes does Aristotle presuppose in the *Rhetorica*? Well, he is clearly an Edenist throughout. He might almost be thought to have invented the Edenist view. As basis of his rhetorical thinking stands a fixed and immutable social reality, "ta . . . upokeimena pragmata," the basic facts. This "real" reality is naturally eloquent and convincing. "The basic facts, things that are better and truer, are always easier to prove and to believe" (1355a). Reality is always better than appearance ("ta pros alētheian tōn pros doxan," 1365b). And, since the real self is the central self, "What a man wants to *be* is better than what a man wants to *seem*, for in aiming at that he is aiming more at reality," the two opposed verbs here being *einai* and *dokein*. When he approaches style at the beginning of Book 3, the Edenic premises come strongly to the fore. About style we must first know that argument from the facts themselves ("auta ta pragmata") comes before clothing facts in language (1403b). Rightly ("dikaion") we ought to argue our case from the facts alone ("autois agōnizesthai tois pragmasin," 1404a). Rightly, that is, language ought to be perfectly transparent, have no effect at all on "the facts themselves." Aristotle realizes, of course, that things seldom are constituted "rightly." Considerations of style cannot help having a small effect ("to mikron anagkaion") due to the infirmity of the hearers, but, he hastens to add, this is not so important as we often think. The word he uses for *infirmity* ("mochthēria") has a strong moral flavor, leaning from weakness toward wickedness, and sets us up for what amounts to a wholesale condemnation of rhetoric itself.

Then comes the famous remark about rhetoric and geometry. The Rhys Roberts translation, which is my regular crib, renders it this way: "All such arts [the arts of language ("to . . . tēs lexeōs")] are fanciful and meant to charm the hearer. Nobody uses rhetoric when teaching geometry" (1404a10). We come here upon a root assumption of fundamental significance. A world "rightly" constructed, and not full of "weak-to-wicked" hearers, would not need style, and hence rhetoric, at all. The Edenic premise which Aristotle adopts abolishes style, and rhetoric, altogether. He presents himself, that is, as writing a treatise about a subject which really ought not to exist at all. Thus begins the long and depressing bad conscience about rhetoric, and style, which has colored rhetorical theory ever since. In the Edenic world, to teach someone about rhetoric, how to use words self-consciously, means teaching him how to be insincere, how to lie, how to sin. And no amount of Ciceronian wind about the orator as nature's polymath has ever succeeded in dispersing this cloud.

The giveaway to Aristotle's thinking comes in the allusion to geometry. He is talking about how language reflects social reality. His example of *ideal* social reality is *geometry*. The strong Platonic bias Aristotle started out with really shows through here. The facts of social reality, rightly considered, are just like the facts of geometry. They have the same existence independent of man and are known in the same way. From this premise, usually unmentioned or, as in this passage, emerging as an inadvertent aside, devolves the fundamental contradiction in Western thinking about rhetoric: rhetoric accepts as its main premise a theory of social reality which directly contradicts its own reason for being. From Aristotle on to the American flowering of C-B-S pedagogy, rhetoric will continue to pull the rug out from beneath its own feet, to argue that its fundamental truths are all truths about a false world. From here on, the better rhetoric gets, the worse it becomes. And the more practically useful its advice, the more it will ignore or contradict its fundamental operating premise.

Aristotle is neither exempt from these difficulties nor totally unaware of them. Having gotten his Edenic premises and pieties down pat, he then goes on to tell us how to behave in a Post-Darwinian world. You can see it happen in the passage which immediately follows the aside about geometry. The Rhys Roberts translation, remember, went this way: "All such arts are fanciful and meant to charm the hearer. Nobody uses rhetoric when teaching geometry." Roberts is, like almost all modern translators of classical Greek, a stalwart Edenist (this is a major problem in talking about Greek rhetoric and about Plato too), and he often makes Aristotle seem even more Edenic than he is. So it is here. A Post-Darwinian translator would come up with a markedly different emphasis. "All such arts are fanciful" translates "apanta phantasia taut'" and "meant to charm the hearer" translates "pros ton akroaten." But this latter phrase means literally "to the hearer," and "phantasia" often means not "fanciful things" but something more like what we might call the creative imagination. So the Approved Post-Darwinian Translation reads: "But these traits of style are all affairs of the creative imagination and depend for their effect on addressing the hearer, so that no one need use them in teaching someone how to do geometry." Here the possibility opens up that social facts, social reality, may *not* be exactly like geometrical reality. I think that a number of passages in the *Rhetoric* could be translated in this way, so as to expose a fundamental ambivalence. In fact, I would be willing to argue that the whole *Rhetoric* is ambivalent in this same way. Aristotle proceeds from Edenic premises, but these constantly turn into Post-Darwinian ones and back again. Aristotle does not seem to be aware that he is working both sides of the street, though it often makes laughable the "logic" of his argument, and he certainly nowhere confronts the issue directly. We can see this queasy ambivalence working outrageously in the passage (1404b) immediately following this one.

First, we are told that a style must be clear ("lexeōs aretē saphē einai") since language doesn't do its job if it doesn't make clear what object the words are a sign of. Both the words Aristotle uses, "dēlos" and "saphēs," point directly to a transparent style, unnoticed and ideally evaporative before the objects it indicates. But then he segues to a less transparent conception of language and a less geometrical conception of social reality. A style must not only be clear, it must be *appropriate,* neither too base ("mēte tapeinēn") nor too highfalutin ("mēte uper to axiōma") but decorous ("alla prepousin"). *Decorum* provides a classic case of the ambivalence I have just been discussing. It can refer, for its fitness, either to an external object, as in the

geometry example, or to a *social situation,* in which case the fitness
will be of a completely different kind. Next we are told that the
language of poetry does not fit prose. Prose must use everyday words.
So we are back to a C-B-S theory again, with its fixed external reality
and neutral language-user. But then we are told that people are
interested in unusual things and so we must give our everyday speech
an un-everyday cast, a foreign air ("poiein zenēn tēn dialektōn").
Since such effects are permissible in poetry but, as he has just said,
not acceptable in prose, in prose you must use them carefully, hide
them. The conclusion to all of this comes in another famous passage:

> For these reasons, a writer must hide his art, and seem to write
> naturally ["pephukotōs"] rather than with preparation. For naturalness
> is persuasive and artificiality is not, since it makes our readers smell
> a trap, as if we were mixing their wines for them.

Here, in this magnificent non sequitur, we have left the Edenic,
geometric social reality far behind and taken the ferryboat right over
to Post-Darwinia. This is truly the Flanders-and-Swann advice to
"Always be Sincere, whether you mean it or not." The virtue and
candor and truth which a few pages before were so naturally persuasive
now need a little help from their friends. Aristotle advocates here
precisely the *artificial* naturalness that was to dominate so much
Renaissance thinking about style under the name Castiglione invented
for it in *The Courtier, sprezzatura.* And *sprezzatura* describes a dramatic
reality, the kind they have in Post-Darwinia, not in Eden.

Aristotle has here, in about thirty lines, sketched out the fundamental
inconsistency that has plagued Western rhetorical thinking and teaching
from his time to ours. You start out with an Edenic C-B-S theory
and, as it becomes more and more obvious that it will not work,
you add epicycles to it, and epicycles to those epicycles, until, without
realizing it yourself or admitting it to anyone else, you have completely
changed your ground, bought your ticket to Post-Darwinia and ridden
right over in a fit of absence of mind. You now dwell in a world
where imposture *creates* social reality rather than dissolving it, but
no matter, you just shut your eyes and keep muttering the Edenic
C-B-S platitudes. Aristotle, fearful, I suppose, lest he has not given
poets as much ground for confusion as he has allocated to orators,

goes on to rehearse the same epicyclical nonsense for metaphor, telling us that it bestows both naked clarity and self-conscious charm, and that, though its use cannot be taught, he will go on and teach us the rules for using it anyway.

I will not carry you through the discussion of metaphor step-by-step, but my main point cannot be sufficiently stressed. Writing has been taught from the same self-contradictory premises ever since Aristotle's radical misunderstanding. And until we get straight just what conception of self and society, and therefore what conception of motive, we are operating under when we teach writing, we will continue to undermine the grounds of our own argument. In the long span from Aristotle to ourselves the writers who saw the problem can be numbered on one hand. Only with the Renaissance thinking that Castiglione both summarized and enfranchised did the issue attract general interest. And even then the proleptic shade of Bishop Spratt lurked in the wings, and the tradition speedily returned to the Aristotelian self-contradictions. It remains to be seen whether in our own time, surrounded by a Post-Darwinian reality pouring in on us from every art and practically every learned discipline, we will get the matter straight even now, or remain the only Edenites in a Post-Darwinian world, the last Ptolemaic astronomers. When, and only when, we do get our sense of self and society straight will we have a genuinely New Rhetoric.

The readjustments required to move beyond Eden to a genuinely Post-Darwinian perspective, a really "New Rhetoric," are radical in the literal sense. They reach to the roots, to the meaning of fundamental terms like appearance and reality, "doxa" and "alētheia," as Aristotle calls them. Let me, for one illustration of this, glance at the least controversial corner of the *Rhetoric,* Aristotle's division of oratory into political, legal, and epideictic styles. This discussion, which occurs in Book 1 (1358a-b), has prejudiced the case ever since. From an Edenic perspective, remember, people always do things for practical purposes. They choose, as Aristotle says a bit later (1366a), actions that lead to the realization of their ends ("ta pros to telos"). It seems obvious enough, doesn't it? But what of that Post-Darwinian behavior-for-its-own-sake? What of rhetoric for the sake of the contest, argument for the pleasures of contention? We know, of course, that both of

these things were very common, perhaps even predominant, in Aristotle's Greece. Epideictic oratory, display oratory for its own sake,
is often deplored by modern commentators as "oratorical inebriation"
(George Kennedy), but the category included Pericles' funeral oration
as well as Gorgias's more inebriated efforts in the same genre. Aristotle
here does not even consider these nonpurposive ranges of motive.
The oratory of display is made simply an affair of praising and blaming,
placed in a wholly purposive framework, one not the less beguiling
for being unacknowledged. And the competitive and playlike elements
in political and legal oratory are similarly ignored, defined out of
existence. Again, of course, having set up this Edenic paradigm, he
goes on to modify it by epicycles lest it seem too hopelessly inapplicable
to real life. (People do argue for victory, he remarks in 1370b.) But,
as in the discussion of style, the damage has been done. Ideally, all
oratory is purposeful, and thus the West inherits, in just the same
way that it inherited Aristotle's bad conscience about style, his bad
conscience about arguing to win, about speaking for fun, about talking
just to keep the social drama going.

This illusion of purpose as the whole of human motive leads Aristotle—and again the rest of us—into misunderstanding the purpose
not only of epideictic oratory, but of legal and political oratory as
well. To see how, consider for a moment the Anglo-Saxon theory
of jurisprudence. What "really happened" in a case—what Aristotle
would call "auta ta pragmata"—is not decided by a magistrate who
scientifically sifts the evidence, as in the Continental system. The
"facts," in our system of jurisprudence, are divined by a ludic struggle,
by a proceeding that is highly social. The "truth" is arrived at by
going *through* strife and emotion, not by outlawing them. Thus a
lawyer who thinks only of his client's interest can genuinely claim
to be acting justly, since he plays his part in a drama which *establishes*
what is accepted as social reality. And we can say the same thing,
in our democratic political system, for the uses of political oratory.
What is accepted as political "reality" emerges from a process in
which strife and pure play loom as large as "the issues" themselves.
Intellectuals usually deplore this and maunder on about "the issues,"
since they are inveterate Edenites, but the system, much wiser than

they, accommodates the whole range of human motive, game and play as well as purpose.

A democratic "justice" as well as a democratic "social reality," then, is Post-Darwinian rather than Edenic. True for us, this was doubly true for classical Athens. And, as many other sections of the *Rhetoric* make clear, Aristotle saw this and came to terms with it. But he never really understood it. The Edenic premises stood in his way. And, again, he has bequeathed his misunderstanding to us, so that we Edenically simplify both the language and behavior of politics and the language and behavior of jurisprudence.

Thus, more than a theory of style, or even a verbal pedagogy, hangs upon our developing a genuinely new, Post-Darwinian, rhetoric. To redefine rhetoric is to redefine politics as well, and hence our conception of social reality. Our suspicion of style, of "fancy language," comes from the same misunderstanding as our suspicion of politicians. We think they are *making up* "reality." They are. We all are. And in the same way that we make up ourselves, by social drama. We cannot remain self-conscious about this all the time, obviously, as Hamlet found out. We find our way around in the world not by scientific facts ("ta pragmata") but by stylistic intuition. Style, verbal or behavioral, constitutes what we need to think an unfakeable code. We need to think it unfakeable because, if the social drama is to proceed, we simply don't have time to test it for fakery. And since this is so, we don't *want* to look too closely, to become self-conscious either about words or behavior. And yet we must, if we are to get our own act together. We must resolve Aristotle's irresolution. We must return, as they have done in Post-Darwinia, to the root paradox, the self-conscious and rehearsed natural spontaneity that Castiglione called *sprezzatura*. Only in these terms can the epicycles of C-B-S rule-making—the style that is familiar and yet strange, visible yet not noticed—make any sense. It is a Renaissance commonplace that only artifice is natural to man, but in the teaching of rhetoric we have yet to learn what this commonplace really means. We remain, like Aristotle, so beguiled by the illusion of purpose that we cannot see, and use, the purposes of illusion.

Chapter 3
The Choice of Utopias:
More or Castiglione?

Santayana, in the "Later Soliloquies," offers two polar definitions of freedom: "the liberty of liberalism" and "German freedom." "German freedom," he tells us, "is like the freedom of the angels in heaven who see the face of God and cannot sin. It lies in such a deep love and understanding of what is actually established that you would not have it otherwise; you appropriate and bless it all and feel it to be the providential expression of your own spirit."* Against this Nixon-team-player paradise he sets a liberty of liberalism which "consists in limiting the prescription of the law to a few points, for the most part negative, leaving it to the initiative and conscience of individuals to alter their life and conversation as they like, provided only they do not interfere with the same freedom in others."† But the modern liberal, especially in recent chiliastic moods, obviously feels the pull of "German freedom" too. He wants to enself the larger polity, inhabit a society whose interests he expresses spontaneously as his own. Modern liberalism might, in fact, be defined as the assumption that we can enjoy the advantages of both freedoms with the disadvantages of neither. The ups and downs of liberal democracies suggest that this homogenized heaven does not come easy. The two freedoms vary inversely, not concomitantly. In a state where "compulsory service" becomes "perfect freedom," it is the individual who withers away, not the state. The game they play is zero-sum.

More's *Utopia* has earned its sacred niche in the humanist pantheon by camouflaging this unhappy fact. It fools us in exactly the way we want to be fooled. In both feelings and ills felt, *Utopia* foreshadows—maybe we should say founds—the basic self-contradiction of modern humanism. More had, of course, an immense stroke of luck. His martyrdom made him not only a saint but a secular Socrates redivivus whom we tremendously *want* to believe. This numinous penumbra,

---

* George Santayana, "German Freedom," in *Soliloquies in England and Later Soliloquies*, intro. by Ralph Ross (Ann Arbor, 1967), pp. 169–73; the quotation is from p. 169.

† "Liberalism and Culture," in ibid., pp. 173–78; the quotation is from p. 174.

as yet undissipated,* obscures how *Utopia* really works, how it manages to reconcile the mighty political opposites. More works this reconciliation by a scam, and since we are still building our vision of social paradise on the same trick, it may yet be useful to see how More brings it off.

Utopia works in two ways, through argument and through literary structure, and these two ways stand fundamentally opposed. The argument offers an either/or choice, not a reconciliation. About this choice, the historian J. H. Hexter has made the definitive statement:

> Here, I think, lies the heart of the matter. Deep in the soul of the society of More's day, because it was deep in the soul of all men, was the monster Pride, distilling its terrible poison and dispatching it to all parts of the social body to corrupt, debilitate, and destroy them. . . .
>
> The Utopian Discourse then is based on a diagnosis of the ills of sixteenth century Christendom; it ascribes those ills to sin, and primarily to Pride, and it prescribes remedies for that last most disastrous infection of man's soul designed to inhibit if not to eradicate it. For our understanding of the Utopian Discourse, it is of the utmost importance that we recognize this to be its theme.†

More originally embodied this theme in the island-paradise vision which, in the final *Utopia,* Raphael Hythlodaeus delivers as Book 2. But later, according to Hexter's brilliantly convincing reconstruction of *Utopia*'s textual history, More added another section, most of the present Book 1, as a broad social critique of European society. Thematically, if Pride is More's main target, Book 2 follows naturally from Book 1. We have in the first the diagnosis, in the second the cure. And the "Dialogue of Counsel," the section in Book 1 where the usefulness of courtly service to a prince is debated, fits perfectly. The debate has two real sides, but the nays seem to carry the day. For More, as for Marx, conventional politics were doomed to inconsequence precisely because man was dominated by Pride. If they

* G. R. Elton has, however, taken a step in this direction with his brilliant "Thomas More, Councillor (1517–1529)," in *St. Thomas More: Action and Contemplation,* ed. R. S. Sylvester (New Haven, 1972), pp. 87–122.

† J. H. Hexter, *More's "Utopia"; The Biography of an Idea* (New York: Harper Torchbook ed., 1965), pp. 75 and 76–77.

were not, why had they not accomplished something before now, why allowed the present abuses? In its diagnosis that man's central ailment is Pride, Utopia becomes a homogeneous whole. It was, of course, in order to extirpate Pride that Plato, in the *Republic,* had invented the German idea of freedom in the first place.

But what, when you denounce Pride, do you really outlaw? We can profit here from a terminological revision. Pride is obviously a loaded word, a Christian vice, but the concept emerges from a deep Platonic paradox. The *Republic* argues for a hierarchical society but a frozen one. Ordinary folk were not to become self-conscious about social status and begin to look aloft. Hierarchy was necessary, but it must be stable. Hierarchy, however, is by nature unstable. The bottom always wants to be the top. The naturally stable social form is equality. The *Republic* united the two by positing a hierarchy whose *ruling class* would be egalitarian. More faced the same basic problem but he could not adopt the same solution, however special a case he made for the scholars. It smacked too much of pride, for one thing, and it too much resembled the Tudor status quo for another. What to do? He separated the hierarchical impulses into separate strands. The elements that conduced to peace and stability—the basic family structure, respect for old age, a modicum of political power—would be preserved, but the central offender, the as-we-now-know basic male primate urge for social status, would be banished. In Tudor terms, this meant the chivalric cluster. More saw it clearly as the heart of the matter. So in Utopia there would be no hunting, no knightly war, no courtly love (the courtship aspect of male status-competition).

More's satire here corresponds exactly to Thorstein Veblen's in *The Theory of the Leisure Class.* Everything that leads to invidious comparison must go, and go in the name of plain purpose. Food is for nourishment, marriage for children, housing for shelter, clothing for warmth. Plain purpose is the only kind of motive Utopia permits—except, of course, for the scholars. Now when you banish invidious comparison, you banish a great deal, as More and Plato saw. (Veblen, whose utopianism was of the temperamental beatnik variety, did not.) The arts must go. Since the only range of motive permitted is the plain purposes we are all supposed to share, individualism must go. And along with both, as a consequence, you must banish *style,* the formal machinery by which we express individual differences, the ornamental behavior by which we dramatize status. Play, too, must go. And—remember Utopian euthanasia and premarital sexual inspections—sentiment as well. And dramatic motive, our role-playing selves. And reality-maintenance behavior, all the activities which have as their end not plain purposes but only proving to ourselves that we are still alive, that the social encounter group of life remains in session. All these add up to an enormous price to pay for social stability.

The term *Pride* disguises this price. We can have, for example, "justifiable" pride, "real" status, "genuine" difference. The way More chooses to construct Utopia shows that he recognized what "Pride" disguised, how much would in fact have to be given up. Popes, he knew, were "proud" in the same way kings were. If More outgrew the confusions of the term, so should we. Let me substitute two less weighted ones. Let's call the behavior utopia admits *purposive* and the behavior it excludes *stylistic.* Of course, *purposive* behavior has its stylistic element and *stylistic* behavior its own purposes, but it was just these overlaps which More was concerned to disentangle.

A rigorous and uncompromising choice, then. But the literary structure does not reflect or intensify this choice. It moves in the opposite direction. Michael Holquist has argued that the utopia, as a genre, lacks literary interest.* Precisely such interest More sought to supply in the revision. Hexter has so cogently reconstructed and accounted for this revision in historical and biographical terms that we tend to overlook the basic alteration in literary structure which the added material brought with it. This alteration serves, in little and large, to blur the conceptual choice between style and purpose.

To Hythlodaeus's utopian monologue in Book 2, More prefaces the dialogue of Book 1. Dialogue suggests a truth both tentative and socially determined which counterbalances the absolutism of Utopia and of Hythlodaeus's monologue about it. Yet, since the section added in London details the abuses to which Utopia supplies satiric answers, Book 2 seems to follow inevitably from Book 1, rather than contrast with it. It is often remarked that Book 1 offers dramatic characterization

* "How to Play Utopia: Some Brief Notes on the Distinctiveness of Utopian Fiction," *Yale French Studies* 40–41 (1968): 106–23.

lacking in Utopia itself. True, but not really the main point. The *kind of* self Book 1 depicts would not occur in Utopia, yet More, through his narrative structure, makes it seem otherwise. The intense self-consciousness of the humanist circle More takes such pains to depict would never develop in Utopia but seems to dwell there nevertheless.

So too with More's humanist Latin. Humanist Latin stands for the central Christian humanist effort to save the world by a stylistic *paideia.* It enshrines all the stylistic virtues of a literary culture which, in the name of clarity and plain purpose, would most certainly have to be banished from a consistent Utopia. It sneaks into Utopia by the back door precisely what More banishes through the front—style and all that it represents. (I cannot pursue here a rhetorical analysis of More's style, relevant as it would be. Elizabeth McCutcheon's detailed analysis of litotes in *Utopia* shows how extensive such an analysis would have to be and the interesting results it would certainly yield.* More was obviously writing a self-consciously ornamented Latin. He was using the devices of literary style to urge upon us a Utopia where such devices—like literature itself—could have no place.

The banishment of money works in a similarly oblique way. It is money which allows us to convert naive purpose into stylistic behavior without anyone else's knowing it. Including ourselves. Money represents the perfect practical purpose. No one has to explain why he wants to get rich. Everyone thinks greed the most hardheaded of motives. And yet the rich man immediately begins to play. It is not the impersonality of money that muddles human relations, as a modern economist might argue, but the way it allows us to shift from one kind of motive to the other. More saw this clearly, and so money had to go.

Minor details often work in a subliminal way too. More tells us, for example, that the Utopians have fools—the professional kind. If we pause to think about it, the Utopians have no more need for fools than for the comedy they represent, for both are generated by the stresses of an open society. But we don't pause to think about it. We accept it as seemingly inconsequential detail and then *assume,*

* "Denying the Contrary: More's Use of Litotes in the *Utopia,*" *Moreana* 31–32 (1971): 107–21.

on the basis of it, that Utopia includes the social stresses that generate comedy and make it necessary—the stresses of an open society. In the same way, in a society like Utopia, those emeriti professors, when not playing king, would have no occasion to sit around pondering the nature of goodness, evil, human happiness, and so on. These ruminations are remnants left over from the open society of a fallen world, but More needs them to effect his reconciliation of utopias. Like the fools, they imply that Utopia possesses the atmosphere and pleasures of the open society while at the same time remaining fully closed.

More drags in other details from the non-Utopian world with a similar intent, to provide ligatures between the two worlds, air-ducts which the reader will never notice. The character of Hythlodaeus, as an obvious example, takes form in Book 1. He is a man of peace, shrewdness, and good will. Thus, when he comes to describe Utopia with such glowing approval, we assume it to be peaceful, shrewd, and kind too, else he would not feel so at home there. And More had taken pains at the beginning of Utopia to introduce Hythlodaeus as a real person, one with whom he and Peter Giles shared that private world of Latin humanism to which the prefatory letters attest. The Utopian island is a different kind of place yet in the same world, or Hythlodaeus could not have gone there. So, too, the Utopians not only read Sophocles, they read him in the edition with the small Aldine type. So, too, in the much-remarked political overlap with Christianity, of which we again overlook the central significance: an unfallen world like Utopia would not need or understand a religion based on a myth of the Fall. But such an inconsistency doesn't matter. As long as we keep debating the doctrinal significance of this overlap, we shall never notice—as the commentary proves—its literary significance, the opening of another duct to let open air into a closed society. Nor do we notice what is implied by the banishment of lawyers, perhaps the most obvious of these dogs that do not bark. A lawyer-class that would never have arisen must be banished to establish yet another presumption for a kind of atmosphere Utopia would never have permitted.

Thus the *Utopia*'s literary form does more than provide dramatic interest, drawing the reader from his chimney-corner. It allows More to suggest and get credit for an open society, to make us feel that he understands the values of one, without formally admitting such a society to his argument. The greatest artist of this con game is Plato, but More follows not far behind. Plato's rhetorical stratagem for hiding totalitarian thinking was a central protagonist who bragged incessantly about his open-mindedness. More does something similar in the *Utopia* by inventing the fictional More who may not be the historical More, and the Hythlodaeus who really may be. Modern commentators have vexed themselves about what More really thought, not unduly perhaps but in the wrong way. *Utopia*'s literary structure does indeed, as has often been noticed, make us read deep and hard, poses for us not More's answer but More's choice. But it also makes the commentators rehearse by their own disagreements the impediments More saw to the political stability of the open society. Making us ask, "What did *More* think?" is a rhetorical trick to make us realize that such an open society can never agree on where to go and so can never arrive there.

What More has done stands clear enough. His reconciliations between the two kinds of freedom, two kinds of society, are all literary. Like the character of Hythlodaeus himself, they smuggle the stresses, virtues, and pleasures of an open society into a closed one which, logically, could never tolerate them. In the context of this overall rhetorical strategy More's tone and wit begin to make sense. Hexter points out that whimsy and playfulness come not, as we would expect, in the Dialogue, but in the Discourse,* not in Book 1 but in Book 2. They come, that is, in the context where they do not belong, a context which would never by itself have generated them. Hexter explains this difference as a *historical* one, but it is obviously formal too, and perhaps even more significant in its formal than its historical aspect.

Utopia thus aims to reconcile Santayana's two humanisms, but it never makes a point of this reconciliation. Just the opposite. It makes a point of never making a point of it. The commentary of *Utopia* often makes it seem as if it *does not have* a literary form, as if it rings true to Holquist's type. But the opposite case prevails. *Utopia* offers us a literary reconciliation while posing an intellectual choice. Its

---

* *Utopia,* The Yale Edition of the Complete Works of St. Thomas More, vol. 4, ed. Edward Surtz, S.J., and J. H. Hexter (New Haven, 1965), p. cxxii.

style and structure, its literary form, aim to reconcile stylistic and purposive behavior. *Utopia* as a utopia insists, in the most uncompromising way—scholars excluded—that these two ranges of motive can *never* be reconciled and that, if we want peace and quiet, we must choose the purposive Utopia and banish the stylistic one. This choice is the only one, and it can be posed in no other way. *Utopia* offers us this choice in the most tough-minded manner—and then implies, through its literary form, that finally we need not make it. It uses style to repudiate style. It assumes as constants all the desirable things stylistic behavior creates and assigns to stylistic behavior only the destructive ones. It does, that is, what humanism has tried to do ever since. It offers the best of both possible worlds and the worst of neither. No wonder it has been so popular.

In *Utopia*, if not in Utopia, we can be equal and yet individual, preserve the pleasures of style *and* the pleasures of renouncing it, take no thought for the morrow yet harvest the deserved crop of forethought. David Bleich has argued* that Utopia constituted a wish fulfillment for More: More really wanted to be king, thought he could invent a better England and rule it better than Henry VIII; Utopia resolved the inner stresses of his private life—his need to provide for a large family, serve God and Wolsey too, attain the sexual satisfaction Dame Alice failed to provide. Bleich is probably right. Utopia seems an embarrassingly personal utopia. Yet the really significant wish-fulfillment is ours and *Utopia*'s, not More's and Utopia's, so that *we* should be embarrassed too—"we" as men of liberal good will who have reconciled a literary *Utopia* with a conceptual utopia; and "we" as scholars, because it was as a scholar that More fooled himself as well as the rest of us. In the scholarly arguments, More caught himself off guard. The scholars are allowed true leisure. They are allowed *play*, the play of the mind, and this (witness the humorlessness of Teutonic scholarship) will always stand at odds with German freedom and will, if continued, always bring it down.

The flinch here reenacts the basic scholarly self-delusion, a Utopia embarrassingly like the "Good-Guys U." we all daydream of. As scholars, we are all natural conservatives. We want a surrounding

* "More's *Utopia*: Confessional Modes," *American Imago* 28, no. 1 (Spring 1971): 24–52.

society that stays still and lets us get on with our work. Bursts of religious zeal may overpower us, as the campus disruptions proved, but they don't last. Our minds move naturally in the other direction. We want the German kind of freedom because it depends on *Kultur* (I am borrowing again from Santayana), and making and retailing Kultur constitutes our basic business. At the same time, we value the free play of the mind, knowledge "for its own sake," stylistic behavior in its purest form. Such behavior, we are sure, will prove in the end the most *purposive* of all. We don't want to think through the inconsistencies of our position. That would interrupt our work and might prove too piercing. And thus we assume that what we want to be so, *is* so, and when a document like *Utopia,* written by one of us, comes along to tell us we are right, we clutch it to our bosoms. And if, being good scholars, we ask it many questions, we make sure not to ask it the embarrassing ones.

But now we must. Our humanism cannot be based on this amiable self-delusion any longer. For it is just the failure to outgrow More's categories and diagnosis that has condemned modern humanism to its present aimless disarray and growing inconsequentiality. Because we have failed to find the true legitimating premises of humanism, we cling to More's sleight-of-hand. We cling especially to his *diagnosis* of social evil, to finding the *principia malorum* in pride. What "Pride" includes, what More excludes from Utopia, amounts to nine-tenths of human behavior. We must abjure not only the status games we like to play, but play itself. Hexter remarks that in Utopia "there are practically no adiaphora, practically no things indifferent":* no loose ends, no goofy hobbies, nothing done for its own sake, no collectors because no objects to collect. No one wastes his time working around the house—how totally More has designed Utopia as a scholar's paradise—because the houses, all the same to begin with, get swapped every ten years anyway. No one can get interested in clothes either, since everyone goes around in Peking unismocks. Scholars seldom ask what Utopia would be like if you did *not* like to study. Not only forbidden to spend your leisure as you wish—no racetracks, card-parlors, or bars—unless you were one of Utopia's professional graduate

---

* *Utopia,* ed. Surtz and Hexter, p. cxv.

students, you wouldn't be allowed much real leisure anyway. Academics seldom see this as a problem—Utopia is, after all, an *academic* paradise—but the lower orders would surely be hard pressed for entertainment.

More's Utopia models perfectly the satiric simplification of human nature. The satirist plies his trade by singling out for scorn the non-purposive, playful, stylistic behavior mankind so likes. The premise is More's premise, the great unexamined one. The satirist assumes that man is fundamentally a purposive creature, that his behavior possesses, or should possess, a fixed purposive center. His whole conception of "reason" and of "reasonable" behavior exfoliates out from this fixed center. Satire depends on the Fall-of-Man myth that in Platonic or Christian form has dominated Western thinking from the beginning. The myth of the Fall establishes man as by nature unselfconscious and purposive. His stylistic motives, his ornamental impulses, are aberrations. This distinction inheres in our language; our terminology focuses human nature in this way. If we banish all ornament, for example, we cannot wholly repine, because ornament and ornamental behavior—the very word *ornament* tells us—do not really matter, they take us away from the center rather than toward it.

The satirist, like More, assumes that man possesses a fixed central self which society can influence but which it does not create. Thus the whole range of stylistic behavior—the social drama which allows us to reenact ourselves, to keep the self alive by social rehearsal—becomes frivolous and dispensable. Serious people need not bother with it. Utopia abolishes it.

In doing so, although we shrink from admitting it, Utopia also abolishes man—a cure indeed worse than the disease. The Western Eden, by excluding Pride, has always dismissed most of human behavior. Our continual fixation upon such a drastically simplified paradise poses one of the most interesting questions in Western intellectual history. Western man has always wanted to deny his essence, pretending to be a different creature from what his history and his common sense reveal him to be. Perhaps this is why we so like satire. The more it castigates us, the more it flatters us by its implication that we are, at heart, the purposeful, serious, unselfconscious, unplayful beings we would like to be and—in Utopia—become. If this delusion were only daydreaming, it would do little harm. But it does do harm. Utopias define for us, albeit often in an indirect way, where we are going or would like to go. They define our essence. And Western man, by thinking that eliminating style takes him toward the center of experience rather than away from it, has systematically deluded himself about his motives. This delusion has made an enormous difference and continues to do so. We have refused to recognize—and hence to make full use of—the principal means of social regulation which we as a species possess. Our fixation on our own purposefulness threatens perpetually to intensify the very problems it seeks to correct.

That the humanities have accepted this purposive Eden must be more surprising still, since the humanities study precisely the stylistic behavior which Utopia abolishes. To put More's Utopia at the center of our humanism is to abolish humanism. This didn't bother More, just as it didn't bother Plato, but it ought to bother us. What happens when we ignore it we are now finding out. We lose our sense of what we are about; our pedagogy for language teaching falls into disarray; we have a composition crisis; the humanities curriculum disintegrates into an intellectual A & P. And when we have to make the choice of choices, ask ourselves—about energy or anything else—what man really needs, we can return no useful discriminations at all, nothing intermediate between Strawberry Fields and a Ferrari in every garage.

The central problem remains More's central assumption, the satiric assumption that all stylistic behavior is "Pride" and all pride, sin. This equation is Marxist as well as Christian, and it can never be reconciled with humanism. Then what happens if we reject it? What happens if we accept as legitimate the stylistic behavior More would banish, or try to control human nature without abolishing it? Well, the Post-Darwinian humanism that I am expounding in this book does just this. It establishes, in fact, a totally different conception of "seriousness" from that upon which More's Edenic paradigm is based, and it provides a choice of utopias beyond the either/or choice posed by More. We can choose a Post-Darwinian utopia.

Such a choice seems a more hopeful one because it is built on the *inclusion* of stylistic behavior, is built, that is, on the whole of man.

When Renaissance scholars continue to accept the Utopia paradigm uncritically, they doom both More's vision and the teaching of Renaissance literature and culture to inconsequentiality. For, after all, More's diagnosis of human motive was as severe as that offered by the Post-Darwinian consensus. He saw the Europe of his own time as dominated, even overwhelmed, by stylistic motive, as predominantly playful and ornamental. To accept his draconian cure—Utopia—as referential and then to interpret the age in its terms means inevitably misinterpreting the age, imposing an anachronistic, purposive motive upon it, repudiating More's *description* of the age and adopting his *cure* as the description. For the most part, this is what has happened. We have taken a purposive view of a stylistically motivated age.

We need not, however, depend on the Post-Darwinian image of man. More's own time was offered the same wider choice of utopias that we face today. *The Prince, The Courtier, Gargantua and Pantagruel*— these works stake out the basic positions, from More's pure purpose to Rabelais's pure play. But one of them demands special attention here because it provides a precise theoretical counterstatement to More's *Utopia*, charts clearly the principal dynamics of what has become Post-Darwinian humanism: it is Castiglione's portrait of Urbino. It chooses the opposite utopia from More's, puts style at the center of reality, not at the periphery. It argues that social stability lies through style, not around it. Society, Castiglione argues, must be self-consciously stylized, literary as well as purposive, if it is to create a self-regulating stability. *The Courtier* charts with the utmost clarity and grace precisely the utopia that modern behavioral science tries to pace out with its seven-league boots of sociologese. Thomas More felt that the two kinds of freedom could be reconciled only within a literary structure. Castiglione accepts this premise but philosophizes it; he creates a *society* which has a literary structure and so permits a genuine reconciliation.

Castiglione seeks not to exclude stylistic motive but to found his society upon self-conscious manipulation of it. No starting-up or stability problems exist. Devising the perfect courtier starts as a game and gradually comes to include ordinary purpose within its boundaries. Castiglione starts from the impulse toward stylistic motive and works outward. The structure of *The Courtier* does not, like *Utopia*, enshrine an absolute choice between conventional politics (*Utopia*, Book 1) and radical politics (Book 2). Instead it moves gradually from a beginning in idle amusement to Bembo's soaring exaltation in Book 4. In between, first one utopia is premised and then the other. All utopias are games, Holquist argues. The Urbino court plays "the best game that could possibly be played," the best because the most flattering, the most narcissistic, the most serious—the game about themselves, about their ultimate values and how they are held. More's rhetorical strategy minimizes our self-consciousness about his literary reconciliation of conceptual irreconcilables. Castiglione does the opposite, maximizing our self-consciousness about his dialogue's domain. It is both purposive and playful by turns, and it deals with a social reality created from a similar oscillation. Over and over it abjures the essentialist position that man has a simple, central, purposive nature and ought to have a single form of society to maximize this nature. As in the beginning of Book 2, so throughout *The Courtier*—all things, defined by their opposites, find their real existence in ordinary behavior in time, not in an ideal pattern standing outside it. We see this most obviously, perhaps, in the famous doctrine of *sprezzatura*, which I alluded to in earlier pages. *Sprezzatura* was a new word for a new conception of identity, that paradoxically natural unnaturalness, sense of effortless effort, of instinctive artifice, that in a static world like More's would simply make no sense. It can work only in a universe anchored in behavior and time, a world where a man can enself a pattern, make natural and spontaneous what was once laboriously learned. *Sprezzatura* stands at the center of Castiglione's conception of human identity, and the rest of Urbino develops out from it. A self based on *sprezzatura* means a self created within society, not preexistent to it, a self created by stylistic behavior, behavior whose purpose is just to dramatize and sustain the self.

At every point, Castiglione embraces the very diversity More would banish. Diversity constitutes his system of social control. Whereas Utopia is a society dominated by rules that aim, finally, to render interpretation otiose, *The Courtier* shows how to create in the citizen intuitive norms that transcend rules. Urbino promulgates no rules for acceptably purposive behavior. The only social corrective is the comic one of reproving laughter, and this depends on a judgment of style. *The Courtier* insists that the norm for human behavior, the potential stability, is created by a balance of the two kinds of motive, purposive and stylistic, and that these can be held together only by a self-conscious society, one that understands and allows both kinds of behavior.

If Castiglione is right, More is wrong. Suicidally wrong. Utopia destroys the social utility of play, the necessary countervailing force to a hypertropic purpose. It shuts down that random variation which, on the level of ideas, it is play's business to introduce.

Let us try, for a moment, to put the problem in evolutionary perspective. We are born with a pattern of plain needs and purposes. We are also born with a primate biogrammar that evolved to cope with needs and purposes which we no longer have and which often conflict with our present ones. These biogrammatical urges make themselves known as play urges, as stylistic behavior. They are so strong that they continually threaten to swamp ordinary purpose. This, More saw happening in his own day. A ceremonial chivalry was eating up the land with its obsessive ritual demands. If ever a purposive corrective has been needed, it was then. But More threw out the principle of regulation with the behavior that needed regulating. We have no reason to think Castiglione less feeling than More or less aware of social abuses. But he did not go for the jugular vein in a paroxysm of indignation and combative zeal. He argued that the mature, self-regulatory culture can, by a judicious use of play, both express and suppress the biogrammar. It will arrange the two kinds of motive and two kinds of behavior in a symbiotic oscillation, one in which purpose is galvanized into action by stylistic motive, and stylistic motive displaced into play when it threatens to destroy purpose. Society, that is, will express for all who live in it the particular scholarly pleasure: thought pursued as play is applied to practical purposes, purposes which in turn generate further thinking-for-its-own-sake. Such a society seems closer to the genuine spirit of the university than Utopia, for all the special status which scholars enjoy there.

But does this balance of motives promise as effective a control of "Pride" and the aggression that comes from it? Better, I think. It moves toward greater dramatic intensity and not away from it, as

Utopia does, and the need for that intensity, a result of an inadequate and inept public drama, generates wars. More says that wars don't just happen; men choose them. He was righter than he knew. Castiglione suggests a more accurate explanation of why we choose them. He also offers a paideia which locates the continuing revivification of human reality in less pathological kinds of behavior than war. The choice of utopias comes down to this: more individualism or less, more self-consciousness or less, more style or less. We stand now in the position opposite to More's, at the end of a long Newtonian interlude of naive purpose. Our threats, in the developed world at least, are more likely to come—as Gregory Bateson has made clear—from the hypertrophy of purpose, not from its opposite.*

We confront again the fundamental contradiction in More's Utopia and in our humanist admiration of it—and in the humanist position in general. Humanists, when they define and defend the humanities, argue that they are useless but essential. With Lear, we cry out, "O reason not the need!" No one gives us an argument about the "useless" but we are often pressed on the "essential" and seldom make much sense of our defense. The business of the humanists is stylistic behavior, nonpurposive behavior. We *feel* this but we do not *know* this. We think that what we do explains much human behavior that otherwise would remain unexplained, but we don't know why. And we never will so long as we still proceed from a Utopian paradigm that considers human behavior essentially purposive.

There is no logical place for humanists in More's Utopia because he has abolished the dimension of behavior it is their job to study. His vision of society as an ideal humanistic community turns out to be just the opposite. It might logically support a technological institute or an agricultural school, but not humanistic learning. And yet we persist in a devotion to the Edenic utopia that is leading us toward a polity very like Utopia's, but one in which we will really pay the price *Utopia* so cleverly disguises. Humanistic inquiry is beginning to pay the price even now, for we remain, in our analysis of motive, as naive as Veblen and as merciless as More. We plan our social

---

* "Conscious Purpose versus Nature," in his *Steps to an Ecology of Mind* (New York, 1972), pp. 426–39.

policy on the basis of a simple-minded purposive conception of human motive and then wonder "why . . . achievements differ so widely from aspirations."*

It is a matter of some moment that the humanists should cease their systematic self-deception and recognize the kind of behavior that constitutes their real object of study. Adjustments will have to be made. We shall have to put aside the "Great Books" obsession that the humanities are to be found in a fixed set of texts, or of subjects. We shall have to redesign the "humanities" course and the "humanities" requirement from top to bottom on the basis of the Post-Darwinian conception of man. The humanist will have to study stylistic behavior wherever it occurs, rather than talking about great books, great ideas, and great art—all generally agreed to be "humanistic." We need to find out about and absorb the redefinition of man that is taking place, often with the most extraordinary originality, in other fields. And we shall have to reinterpret the texts we profess, in order to see if there are other Castigliones who have gotten there first. When we find them, we will really understand them for the first time.

Humanists may, of course, choose to remain with the Utopian paradigm. The "humanities," in that case, will not die. They will, as is happening now, migrate to other fields. And these fields will, in the fullness of time, rediscover the real domain of the arts, the kind of behavior the humanities were invented to describe. Anthropologists will start to use the rules of literary criticism to examine foreign cultures, as Clifford Geertz has done. Ethologists will begin to use rhetorical terms as investigative concepts. Perception psychologists will apply themselves to the history of art. And they will find out what we need to know. But it will be too bad, because we could, as humanists, often handle these problems a great deal better—if only we could decide what utopia really legitimates our enterprise.

When humanists talk about what they are doing, the words *higher* and *lower* often occur. We are trying, we say, to defend the "high" culture against the pop culture, man's higher nature against his lower.

---

* Karl Popper, *The Open Society and Its Enemies,* 2 vols. (Princeton, 1971); the quotation is from vol. 2, p. 95. Popper is a notable victim of the purposive delusion.

Thomas More offers one definition of this distinction: high is purpose, low is pride. I have used Castiglione's brilliant social analysis to suggest that this distinction ought to be reversed. What "high" points to—from fashions to morals—is stylistically motivated, playful not purposive, behavior. Until, as humanists, we see the high culture in these terms—as expressing this definition of man, as choosing this kind of utopia—we will continue to misapprehend the basis of our endeavor. And, thus misapprehending, we will have no right to fuss when our students sense this confusion and leave us, to go where the action is.

Chapter 4
The Chaucerian Biogrammar
and the Takeover of Culture

It would be an exaggeration, but perhaps not so big a one, to argue that disagreements about Chaucer's poetry spin out from one central core—Chaucer's idiosyncratic seriousness, his offbeat version of the earnest/game polarity. And yet we cannot decide just what this distinction meant for Chaucer, what his characteristic conception of human motive actually was. Some critics have addressed the problem directly, Charles Owen for example, but most prefer to go in the back door, to talk about Chaucer's conception of morality and how it differs from our own tattered ethical remnants. This argument about ethics, according to Donald Howard, accounts for 90 percent of the Chaucerian critical conversation. The play/serious polarity surfaces in many other forms, too, discussions of Chaucer's "ambiguity" or "sophistication" or "complexity" or "ironic comedy," which try to explain his irksome habit of never telling us how solemn we ought to feel. This key dualism generates, perhaps, the pattern of "oppositions" that Peter Elbow has found in Chaucer's poetry. And I think, too, that it prompts—to follow yet another recent argument by Robert Burlin—Chaucer's fondness for "mistaking experience for authority or vice-versa, mistaking one fictive level for another or for another mode of discourse or even another reality." This deliberate undermining of seriousness through contextual dislocation, indecorous confusion of levels and types, has troubled Chaucerians for some time. Bertrand Bronson, for example, remarked nearly twenty years ago that "We are not merely disturbed, we are sometimes disoriented and amazed by the rapid shifts of stylistic level, of apparent sacrifice of achieved effects, the reversals of mood and tone, the abrupt stoppage of narrative momentum, the comingling of colloquial and artificial diction, the breathtaking incorporation of the whole range of language into the working texture of the verse." These Ovidian antics seem both to compromise ordinary seriousness and to suggest some other kind.*

* Charles A. Owen, *Pilgrimage and Storytelling in the Canterbury Tales: The Dialectic of "Earnest" and "Game"* (Norman, Okla., 1977); Donald A. Howard, *The Idea of the Canterbury Tales* (Berkeley and Los Angeles, 1976), p. 54; Peter Elbow,

41

Today we stand a little closer to what this other kind of seriousness might be. The process began, for medieval studies at least, with the writings of Johan Huizinga. Not with *Homo Ludens*, though, but with the book that prompted it, the equally famous *Waning of the Middle Ages*. In pondering the paradoxical twilight surface of Burgundian culture, Huizinga came to a revolutionary conclusion. "Life," social reality, was not a homogeneous affair, a constant just "out there," against which art could measure itself. Life varied as much as art, and along the same spectrum of self-consciousness from spontaneous sincerity to sentimental affectation. Life was played. And played hard, and in public. In the medieval fondness for extremes—cruel punishments and absolute pardon, egregious deference and public shame—in the omnipresent pageantry of public life, in the continued force of the chivalric myth, Huizinga saw a culture self-consciously played, a "life" more often than not as "artistic" as art, as "literary" as literature.

The implications of this insight Huizinga addressed in *Homo Ludens*. I intend no depreciation of that remarkable book in saying I agree with Jacques Ehrmann that a fundamental inconsistency runs through it from start to finish. Huizinga never managed to outgrow a normative reality just "out there" and always available for comparison if we wanted to decide whether something was playful or "really serious." Huizinga, Ehrmann argued, considered "'reality,' the 'real,' as a *given* component of the problem, as a referent needing no discussion, as a matter of course, neutral and objective," and he defined play "in opposition to, on the basis of, or in relation to this so-called reality."*
And with this invariant social reality, Huizinga also preserved the central invariant self, that "real me" halfway between the ears, as Erving Goffman puts it, and just behind the forehead. Times are more propitious now for avoiding this fundamental confusion. Perception psychology has reminded us that we construct the world rather than simply look at it. Social role-playing has been a dominant sociological

Oppositions in Chaucer (Middletown, Conn., 1975); Robert B. Burlin, *Chaucerian Fiction* (Princeton, 1977), p. 244; and Bertrand H. Bronson, *In Search of Chaucer* (Toronto and London, 1960), p. 22.

 * *"Homo Ludens* Revisited," *Yale French Studies* 40–41 (1968): 22.

concept for so long that it threatens to slide over into cocktail-party therapy. Our theatre has oozed into the audience, and life has stormed the stage. Oscar Wilde's paradoxes about the supremacy of style have been taken over by the earnestness of Roland Barthes. From happenings and participatory art to nonverbal communication the same message returns to us. We construct our own social reality, construct it as drama, and by playing social roles gradually accrete around ourselves a felt identity, a "real" self.

But if we can see more clearly than Huizinga could in the 1920s, when he was considering these problems, we still make the same mistake. We refuse to think "life" as variable as literature. Chaucer, however, did not make this mistake. His sense of life's literariness creates the characteristic set of his vision. (Hence, perhaps, John Gardner's arguments for his contemporaneity.) He seems, in this respect, far more modern than we are, and the discrepancy between his modernity and our nineteenth-century positivism has created the central critical misunderstanding, the confusion about what is game and what is earnest, what serious and what play. The Chaucerian seriousness will not come into focus until we adopt his root assumption about motive, that it varies in life just as it does in art. What happens when we do adopt it?

To confront the problem in its theoretic entirety would mean to rewrite poetics and rhetoric from Aristotle onward, since assuming "life" as a constant is the central—and mistaken—Aristotelian assumption, both in the *Rhetoric* and in the *Poetics*. (In both, the confusion is fundamental, which is to say terminological. It inheres in the words used—especially in the contrast between "alētheia" and "doxa.") Without tackling the larger project, I would like to suggest just a few areas where, in the Chaucerian context, the problem might be rethought.

We can start with the distinction between "game" and "play." And here, as so often in considering the "literariness" of life, some suggestive perspectives come from ethology and, more recently, from sociobiology. The primary insight, for our misunderstanding of Chaucer, was one that came to Konrad Lorenz early in his career, when he noticed—in a now famous scene—that a pet jackdaw sometimes snapped at nonexistent flies. He also observed that his ducks, when they upended themselves to feed under water, seemed to enjoy the upending for its own sake; to feed for the pleasure of upending rather than the reverse. Ethologists call these spontaneous firings of phylogenetic impulse "vacuum behavior." Such a term may seem a trifle uninspiring, but the concept itself is something else. It suggests for human behavior a genuine wild-card, one we have scarcely begun to consider. If, sometimes or often, we too do things just because we are programmed to do them, just because the behavioral muscle wants to work, then we must account for a kind of behavior which lies altogether outside our customary theories of motive. These theories, various as they are, are all *purposeful*. We do things for particular *reasons*. But if we do things sometimes just for the hell of it, how do we "explain" them "reasonably"? They can be considered leftover evolutionary baggage, but this doesn't take us very far. We can deny, of course, that Homo sapiens reenacts this kind of behavior; we can take a severely culturalist position and argue that we come into the world trailing no clouds of primate hard-wiring whatsoever. This position has been argued repeatedly in the fuss over sociobiology. Whatever evidence can be adduced for it in general, however, it is a hard motival assumption to make about the kind of behavior Geoffrey Chaucer chose to describe. For the irony-centered, game-serious cluster of discontinuities everyone thinks so important in Chaucer's poetry finds its genesis just here—in spontaneous play. The only explanation I have been able to find for spontaneous play is the evolutionary one of vacuum activity. The basic confusion in our Chaucerian conversation, I wish to argue, comes from this behavioral wild-card, spontaneous activity, behavior which emerges even when there is no stimulus— or a manifestly inadequate one—to release it.

We can, to be sure, give this spontaneity a more dignified, high-toned name. Instead of saying that we do something "for the hell of it," we can say—as academics are wont to say of their research— that we are doing it "for its own sake." And we can super-encrypt the spontaneity by enrolling it under one or another purposive banner, pretending that our vacuum behavior took form in the richly oxygenated air of an inspiring cause. But this only disguises the problem, and I do not think Chaucer disguises the problem. Motive again and again in his poetry seems not so much "unreasonable" (reason being purposive) as beyond reason altogether, as just there. Purposive explanations of motive seem to have struck Chaucer as, in varying degrees, ludicrous and irrelevant. He includes them all, to be sure, or at least always a substantial selection. And, to the degree that we think our behavior purposefully motivated, we swallow these proverbial placebos, "take them seriously," argue about "fate" in the *Troilus,* divine justice in *The Knight's Tale,* and so on. Thus is generated that ethicizing 90 percent of Chaucerian commentary. But the real debate ought to concern not *which* ethical principles apply but whether *any at all* apply. This distinction explains, I think, the strand of extreme ethicizing begun by the Robertsonian critique. The issue seems to be not the details of a particular dogma but the relevance of any dogma. Threatened by the total evaporation of conventional ethical seriousness—just the threat Chaucer poses—the complementary extreme defense was inevitable.

It would make things easier if this wild-card behavior were always a *kind* of activity; we could describe and hence sequester it. But it isn't. Instead, it is often a spirit in which we behave, a different way of carrying out usually purposive behavior. We can "play at" anything. And it would make things easier still if we could, in orthodox fashion, simply call this basic human spontaneity "original sin" and have done with it. But this is just what Chaucer's poetry tells us it is *not.* Here again the Robertsonian critique has proved invaluable in focusing the genuine issue. The long and careful reviews that greeted *A Preface to Chaucer* made just our point: to equate this felt yet inexpressible source of motive with "original sin" was not so much to explain Chaucer's poetry as to explain it away, to deny its reason for being. But if so, the ball bounces into the other court. If not a purely purposive conception of motive, a totally ethical seriousness, what then *is* the characteristic Chaucerian seriousness? This question—the obverse of the Robertsonian critique—remains the most important one that Chaucerian criticism has asked itself.

How does vacuum behavior manifest itself in Chaucer's poetry? Have you ever noticed, for a start, how Chaucer's characters very often seem extra ready, primed, for whatever happens to them? They seem ready to play their parts almost before they are offered to them. Troilus wants so badly to do a forsaken-lover-suffering-desperately act that Pandarus has to remind him "Peraventure thou hast cause to singe." Palamon and Arcite, after just the one long-range glimpse of Emelye, almost explode into their sufferings. In both cases the behavior has been released—it does not fire in a vacuum—but in both love affairs Chaucer underlines the *slenderness*, the *fickleness*, of the stimulus. In the case of Emelye, she is hardly there at all, cloned up from rhetorical cliché like Spenser's false Florimell. The *Knight's Tale*, we are reliably informed, is a philosophical romance, but if so the general wisdom it yields seems to be only the extraordinary inconsequentiality of the "motives" which release our behavior. I think this inconsequentiality occurs repeatedly in Chaucer. The ostensible motive seldom seems adequate to prompt the behavior which it in fact releases. And so our endless debates. Why does Walter torment a nice girl like Griselda? Why does hende Nicholas construct so unhende a siege scenario to storm a castle already well in hand? Why is Pandarus so *eager* to pander for Troilus and so *very* eager when he learns that his niece is the lady in question?

Vacuum activity often expresses itself in the sheer gusto with which a character plays his role. Isn't this why we hesitate to condemn the Wife of Bath? Her gusto is vital to life, as we all recognize, and animates our good purposes as well as our bad ones. We may want to condemn the bad purposes but not the gusto, not the propensity to *enjoy* a role. In the Wife, Chaucer gives us one of those dislocations and discontinuities that Bertrand Bronson pointed out. We may sympathize with her feminism or deplore her sexuality, but neither judgment is *like in kind* to our applause for her pleasure in experience per se. That pleasure comes from somewhere else. And, to some extent at least, we can generalize this verdict. If we are by nature social role-players, our sense of *dramatic pleasure* in our role, whatever it may be, is vacuum behavior and hence outside the range of purposeful ethical stricture. The behavior itself may, of course, be dreadful. But the *impulse*, no. Isn't this just the case with the Pardoner?

The sociobiological argument runs this way. Human beings, like other primates, have

> not only a very general physical capacity to learn, they have a programmed preference to learn some things rather than others, and to learn some things more easily than others. It is not *instincts* in

any old-fashioned sense that are at issue here; initiation ceremonies and male rituals are not "instinctive"! They emerge from the biology of an animal programmed to produce them, once it is given the appropriate stimuli. Without these stimuli, there will be no behavior, or only a modified or distorted form of it. The human organism is like a computer that is set up or "wired" in a particular way. It is always in a state of readiness—at successive points in the life cycle— to process certain kinds of information and to produce certain kinds of information.*

To these biogrammatical dictates "we have to yield at least a little or endure a lot" (p. 35). Without arguing the sociobiological case for Homo sapiens in general, I am suggesting that this view fits the Chaucerian Homo sapiens very well. In Chaucerian man, however, the behavioral releasers are filed to a hair trigger. He comes into the world full of propensities, and nearly anything will set these off. And they do very often become distorted in the process. This distortion, furthermore, takes a particular form in Chaucerian man. It goes, in broadest outline, this way. Mankind has invented a culture which aims to control his biogrammar. This culture *governs* the basic bio-grammatical urges—male-female bonding, male-male bonding, mother-child bonding, dominance relationships, and so on. It *controls* these but it does so by channelization and suppression. To take an obvious example, the Christian world-view says that the male-female bond is to be controlled by marriage and other expressions of it are to be suppressed. The control and suppression are exerted in the name of *purpose.* Marriage protects the female who is vulnerable to male desertion, protects the children until they can fend for themselves, and so on. But the wild-card impulse continually struggles against this conception of culture as *suppression* and threatens to turn it into *expression* instead. It threatens to take over culture and play it just for fun. And we don't have the conceptual apparatus, or the terminology, to describe this takeover. Chaucer did not have it, nor do we have it yet. But Chaucer tried to describe this radical mixture in his poetry. (It may be the radical mixture of human culture generally— I think it is—but we need not debate that here.) *His* biogrammar

* Lionel Tiger and Robin Fox, *The Imperial Animal* (New York: Dell, 1974), p. 33.

included the wild-card to a marked degree. Culture was always being taken over by play, and thus taken out of the hands, and the range, of orthodox morality altogether. Serious activities were always being played.

This radically mixed kind of behavior was, I think, what Huizinga saw and tried to describe in *The Waning of the Middle Ages.* It is easy to see why he could not focus it using only a simple reality/play distinction. He could never decide, in *Homo Ludens,* whether play was an *activity* or an *attitude* because, in the life he was examining, as in the Chaucerian biogrammar, it was likely to be first one and then the other, or both at the same time. And it is this continual movement in and out of the domain of conventional ethical seriousness, in both activity and attitude, which generates the characteristic Chaucerian "seriousness." We never know, at any one point, which world we are in. We are always doing—or suspecting that a character is doing—the most serious things just for the hell of it, threatening his, and our, serious life with a radical sentimentalizing, with feeling for its own sake.

Pure play, then, has an innocence that transcends the kind of behavior being played. To judge it requires the kind of split vision, the separating of act and motive, which traditional ethics has always desiderated. We move, though, in the opposite direction, not assessing motive rather than result but assessing result while remembering that motive stands in another domain altogether. This split creates one of the two fundamental Chaucerian displacements. The other comes when vacuum motivation becomes socialized into competition, playing becomes game. Here we have to depart from Chaucerian terminology and establish our own. Play is vacuum activity or such activity elicited in excess of the response, behavior "for its own sake." But behavior like this, as perhaps academics should be the first to recognize, is soon taken over by the ludic impulse. Learning "for its own sake" can quickly become career game. Itself a pronounced vacuum behavior, ludic striving, too, requires a purposive substance to work through. But any will do. Anything can be converted into a game, just as anything can be played out for its own sake. This kind of takeover, especially as seen in the *Canterbury Tales,* by now needs no documentation. The Canterbury pilgrims become poets, and as such they both try to play out their behavior into a poem and also use it to overcome the other poet/pilgrims. We can see this split as an earthly/ heavenly one—one eye on Heaven and the other on winning the prize dinner—but we can just as easily see it as a split between two vacuum motives, play and game, which have taken over the same cultural institution.

In such an interpretation, not much Heaven remains in the whole affair. You can play at pilgrimage and make a game of it, too. One can evaporate the spirituality from the *Troilus* in the same way, Troilus and Criseyde becoming players at the game of love and Pandarus striving to triumph over the forces of private inertia and public circumstance which stand in their way. Or we can think of Pandarus as motivated by play, the pure pleasure of playing his role as Pandar. The eponymous element in both Pandarus and Criseyde urge this motivational weighting to at least some degree, and it evaporates the spirituality of the poem as effectively as before.

The Chaucerian biogrammar, then, finally emerges as offering not a pairing but three possible ranges of motive—play, game, and purpose. Play stands altogether outside the range of conventional morality and game seems half in and half out. Much of the competitive urge, classified as Pride, can be filed under Sin (Unoriginal), but not all. What of the urge which raised the Gothic cathedral vaults ever and ever higher? The root of Chaucer's basic technique, dislocation, is created by relating these ranges of motive. That big 90 percent of the critical conversation centers on how, when, and if we ought to recognize and apply one or more kinds of motive. At one extreme, purpose; at the other, play. Game halfway from the one to the other. You can, given sufficient time and interest, find all the basic Chaucerian literary critical positions in the possible permutations which these three kinds of motive permit.

It is, then, possible to describe Chaucerian seriousness more specifically than heretofore. We must first admit that, for Chaucer, life varied in the same way literature does. When we do admit it and when we put this variation in the only perspective which can contain it, the evolutionary perspective, we see three conceptions of motive as controlling the variation. We can plot these three in *two* ways, and it makes all the difference in the world which way we use. We can, as I have just said, think of play and purpose as opposites on a spectrum like this:

Play	Game	Purpose

Here game is a stage on the way to purpose, a mixed mode. Purpose remains a pure state and so is play. Matthew Arnold would have agreed with this spectrum, though not with where we might place Chaucer's poetry on it. So would most people today. It underlies our conception of ourselves as fundamentally purposive beings. It also underlies most Chaucer criticism. Chaucer, however, wanted it like this:

Play	Purpose	Game

See the difference? A completely different kind of seriousness, not pure but radically mixed. Purposive life becomes a mixture of play and game rather than a kind of behavior specifically purified of them.

As natural spectra, then, for focusing Chaucerian seriousness we have so far discovered (1) life as variable and (2) three kinds of motive that can be arranged in two fundamentally different ways. The first of the two arrangements purifies purpose of play and game; the second suffuses purpose with both. You will recognize, in this choice, an expanded version of the Robertsonian challenge: make play and game equal to sin, choose purpose instead of this sinful kind of motive, and you have that challenge. Accept the other two without defining, or even much thinking about them, and you have all the responses to Robertson, the entire defense of Chaucer's poetry as something—though we are not quite sure what—more than ethical platitude. You have, that is, the current state of the criticism: It won't let life be a variable but won't fix it either.

When we do allow life to vary, and when we accept the mixed Chaucerian seriousness, some consequent difficulties must be faced. The basic Aristotelian terms dissolve, for a start. Nonpurposive behavior renders the beginning-middle-end conception of plot meaningless. It is not that the *Tales* project some "Idea," however incomplete, but that the very concept of completeness comes from a purposive behavior which the *Tales* argue to be tangential. Their basic formal dynamism is that of an aleatory composition, and whether this comes from

Chaucerian design or the force of circumstances doesn't make much difference. The aleatory form stands to vacuum motivation as beginning-middle-end Aristotelian plot stands to purposive behavior. Thus, since vacuum motive dominates the *Tales,* the "incomplete" aleatory form fits its underlying conception of motive perfectly. And so our typical critical response; we are not so vexed by the incompleteness as we feel we ought to be. (The "incomplete" form of the *Faerie Queene* works the same way, incidentally. Northrop Frye's famous essay on its imagery* goes astray in just the same fundamental way that Donald Howard's book on the *Tales* does—in explaining structure on the basis of an alien theory of underlying motivation.)

Characterization, too, dissolves, along with plot, as I argued some years ago,[†] since what we call "character" depends on a purposive theory of motive. But what life as a variable most significantly dissolves for Chaucer is genre and, on a lower scale, metaphor itself. So long as you keep "life" as a control (or, like Aristotle, let it shift around, but don't admit it), you can keep on talking about genre as a *deformation* of normative experience. This obviously will no longer work if life varies, too. A genre can just as well *literally transcribe* a very different kind of experience. Genres, in such a world, all become potential biogrammars, sets of root assumptions about what is *likely to, wants to,* happen in a certain kind of world. Each models a world which we can accept as literally true. We here reverse the experience Clifford Geertz recommends in his brilliant essay "Thick Description."[‡] Instead of considering a foreign culture as a text, we consider a foreign text as a culture, look for and accept its operative rules. These rules will be *biogrammatical,* not conventional.

Let me give you an example. Consider romance and pastoral. If we consider them transcriptions rather than deformations of life, they become perfect models, the one for aggression and the other for submission. The world of romance is built on the territorial premise

* "The Structure of Imagery in *The Faerie Queene,*" in *Fables of Identity* (New York, 1963).

[†] "Games, Play, and High Seriousness in Chaucer's Poetry," *English Studies* (Winter 1967).

[‡] "Thick Description: Toward an Interpretive Theory of Culture," in *The Interpretation of Cultures* (New York, 1973).

that seems, in one way or another, to lie at the base of so much animal behavior. The closer to the territorial center, the more violently the possessor will fight, and the more likely he will win. Such a world assumes antagonism as its initial relationship. So, when two strange knights meet, they must fight to get the status order clear before they can become friends. If we permit life to vary, then romance comes to model a life built on the biogrammar of male status and territorial defense. We can, of course, "verticalize" the territory, transform it symbolically into "spiritual" territory as the *Faerie Queene* does sometimes, but the principle remains the same. Romance, as a "genre" in this sense, does not "conventionalize" experience at all. It seems to deform this central cluster of male status motives simply because it presents them in so clear and concentrated a form. It strips away the ornamental cluster of dogmatic justifications to expose the biogrammar of male hunger for status. And pastoral obviously denies all that romance affirms. Here sexuality is not a derivative of male status, a frantic clustering of young lovelies about the alpha-male, but just the opposite. The premise of social relationship is the gesture of submission, not the aggressive challenge; women become the objects of worship and prayer, not the oldest form of portable property. Again, pastoral in this sense is not a *convention* at all. It is a world built on part of our basic primate biogrammar.

Tapping the biogrammar in this way creates an opposite extreme to generic convention. And, of course, any particular literary text can contain any mixture, offer any degree of interaction between literariness in literature and literariness in life. To borrow for a moment the transparent window metaphor Ortega uses in *The Dehumanization of Art*, we cannot know, at any one time, whether it is the window which is changing or the scene, or what combination of the two. This represents the Chaucerian situation par excellence. Do we see a *neutral*, transparent, literal description of an odd literary reality or a literary, conventionalized picture of a normative reality? Chaucer is continually playing variations on this dilemma. He creates as narrator a "walking literal" who offers a "transparent window" invitation. But he is too obviously a literal, and so Chaucer the poet reenters and the transparent window becomes—another possibility—opaque. He offers a set of characters, pilgrims say, some of whom seem to be—so far as we can tell—certified genuine slices of life. But then he also gives us others, like the Wife of Bath, who seem slices of pure literature, "olde books" literally incarnate but *presented* as slices of life, as their own norm.

The question of genre in Chaucer is always, sooner or later, confused by this continual double variation. From one point of view, every genre he uses *is* a deformation of experience. From another, life itself, the *ipse ille.* So, in the *Troilus,* we are given the courtly code and made to see it, over and over, as a convention. Pandarus sees to this. At the same time the narrator, with a little help from the principals, takes it as a literal transcription of life. Given *two* possible normative realities, we can depend on neither—a perfect multistable puzzle. This sense of permanent potential displacement, so characteristic of Chaucer, is far from easy to manage. That Chaucer succeeds in managing it so well makes a little sad the immense labors of modern critics to undo it, to insist on holding one variable as constant. There sat Chaucer, careful to give every slice of life a literary source, an "olde book," and to make every "olde book" seem naive, a first-time creation. And here we come with our positivistic prejudices and, like a logger with his chainsaw, cut down the trees and then wonder where the forest went.

When genre metamorphoses under the pressures of this second variable, so do some other ancillary Aristotelian concepts. Verisimilitude, for a start. Again, this concept is based on *purpose;* what is *likely* depends on your theory of motive. The coalescence of Western reality around the purposive assumption is very eloquently illuminated by this emphasis on verisimilitude. It does not *want* life to vary; it is just such variation that verisimilitude had been invented to prevent. (This is Eric Havelock's brilliant insight in *A Preface to Plato.*) How insistently Chaucer refuses to abide by verisimilitude! How often the "likelihoods" he uses come from a different range of motive. Palamon and Arcite, for example, offer a motive that, from a behavioral point of view, makes good sense. Their attention opens for a flash and, by a fluke, gets "imprinted" on Emelye. But in the universe of motive where "imprinting" makes sense, perception is not at all purposive. There is no feedback in time or space. Perceptions happen in causal vacuums, discretely, unconnected to one another. They don't make any sense because by *sense* we have learned to mean "purpose." Arranging a battle between two hundred knights because a battle between two knights is too bloody doesn't "make sense" either; nor does making the bigger battle only a ceremonial one, since one of the original two somehow has to get killed, and somehow manages to. And yet, if we literalize the genre, it makes perfect sense. Ritualized combat as a preface to courtship taps a deep biogrammatic program. Homo sapiens too has its leks, its ritual trial grounds where the males show off for the females and are, if they win, rewarded with that wonderful clinical euphemism, "copulatory success." It makes a kind of very good sense even if it makes no sense at all—if, as Theseus says, Emelye doesn't know one hero from another. Both kinds of verisimilitude inhabit the poem, and we have somehow to put them together.

If reality can vary, then, verisimilitude varies in the same way. Everything can be equally "likely," once we find the "reality" that establishes that particular kind of likelihood. Chaucer's game, of course, is always to conflate different likelihoods and leave us to swim among them. We are never permitted for long to keep the same distinction between figure and ground. The central Chaucerian logic is exactly that of the multistable illusion. So Chaucer seems always to ask, in a peculiarly awkward way, what it means to suspend disbelief. For Chaucer, it is not a simple one-time affair. We don't once and for all suspend disbelief, or belief, in anything. We continually oscillate between kinds of belief, alternately accepting the fiction as normative and measuring it against an alien norm. Think what would happen if we did suspend our disbelief for the duration, if, as some modern critical theory argues, literature really did constitute a permanently separate domain of discourse. Such a premise annihilates, for a start, the metaphor on which that same theory is based. By not admitting life as a second variable, you end up—it's, as they say in Hollywood, been done—generating splendid theories of genre that have meaning only when you *do* admit life as a second variable. You end up, that is, outlawing the Chaucerian complexity, and this means outlawing the particular "poetic" complexity, the "poetic" truth, modern thinking has tried so hard to specify. For Chaucer allows only short bursts of belief in any one reality. He saw clearly that to *rest* in a suspension

of disbelief meant accepting that reality totally. And so farewell metaphor, genre, and the rest of it. Your love really *would be* a red rose
and you'd have to construct a world in which this was *always* literally
so.

You could, of course, as in the first part of the *Romance of the Rose*
construct this kind of reality but equip the reader with a set of *reading
assumptions* where the suspension of disbelief was radically qualified.
And, in the traditional fourfold method of allegorical interpretation—
Literal, Allegorical, Moral or Tropological, and Spiritual or Anagogical—
the Middle Ages had just such a set of assumptions. By now we are
deep into the third variable I have been so sedulously avoiding, the
reader's pattern of expectation. Since it can vary in the same way as
the other two, along the same range of motive we have set forth,
and from total belief to total disbelief (i.e., belief in something else)
we face a new set of possible permutations—which I shall not work
through here. Let me remark, though, that the fourfold interpretative
scheme can be transposed into the three kinds of motive I have
discussed earlier. And no one disputes that the fourfold scheme is
present, if not altogether accounted for, in Chaucer's poetry.

We have three variables, then, to bear in mind: our reading behavior,
the poem (the poet's behavior), and the behavior which the poem
imitates. (Notice how even the well-generalized Aristotelian term
imitates tends to prejudice the case?) If these three varied concomitantly,
it would make things simpler. But they don't. Taken together, they
constitute what I have chosen to call the "Chaucerian biogrammar,"
the pattern of inborn tendencies that animate the world we enter
when we read Chaucer's poetry, and the pattern of secondary elab-
orations and discontinuities that result from them. Together, the three
variables provide the boundary conditions within which our experience
will occur. Each of them needs rethinking, and their relationship
especially so. (We shall know we have pushed this rethinking far
enough when we have accounted for all of Chaucer criticism as
embodying one or more of the normative simplifications that this
interpretive framework invites.) What seems truly extraordinary about
Chaucer is the clarity with which he charted the whole range of
variability; how effortlessly he pushed toward, and recognized, the
boundary conditions of literary expressivity. How clearly he saw the

variability of "life," and the need to let it vary, seems perhaps the most remarkable thing of all.

Rethinking the first level of variability would seem, then, to yield a generalization. For Chaucer's Homo sapiens, as perhaps for ours, what compromises the seriousness of human behavior is our very propensity to engage in it. (As Edward Wilson has remarked, "Human beings are absurdly easy to indoctrinate—they *seek* it."* Seriousness, rational purpose, implies a culturalist view of motive. To the degree that we are serious, we must be creatures of culture, not of a phylogenetic biogrammar. Vacuum behavior, on the other hand, and the biogrammatical view of motive which explains it, imply a different kind of seriousness altogether, one whose closest analogue, in conventional critical thinking, would be Bergson's theory of comedy. The debate about Chaucerian seriousness thus finds itself, on the first level, that of life's literariness, exactly modeled in the current sociobiological debate about motive.

As for changes on the second level, our accepted poetics, I hope I have made Chaucer's main point. If we accept the first level, everything on the second is up for debate again and may, in the extreme case, mean the opposite of what we now think it means. To put the matter aphoristically, everything that we now consider substance will become ornament, and everything ornamental will become substantial.†
Chaucer understood from the beginning that every genre is both a temporary verisimilitude and the only kind we are likely to get here below. That is, he saw genre as simultaneously normative and deformative, or at least as in the multistable illusion, first one and then the other. And if this central indicator of verisimilitude could thus vary, so could the rest of poetry and poetic terminology. His self-consciousness about poetry ran as wide and deep as his self-consciousness about reality, and varied along the same spectrum. And of course, witness all his little masks and games with us, he allowed us a similar latitude—if we have the wit to see that it has been offered

---

* *Sociobiology: The New Synthesis* (Cambridge, Mass., 1975), p. 562.

† This reversal is, by the way, the animating principle of Chaucer's use of formal rhetoric. The same reversal provides the rhetorical strategy for a whole tradition that runs from Ovid through Shakespeare to Sterne, as I have tried to show in my book *The Motives of Eloquence* (New Haven, 1976).

and the poise to enjoy it. To do this, to work well and freely on the third level, our level, we must accept the premises of the first, the behavioral level, the discrete ranges of motive, play, game, and purpose that Chaucer saw with brilliant insight as being intrinsic to man. If we can see them in society, we can see how they work in poetry and in poets, and from there how they work in ourselves. We will always stop temporarily on one level, in one range of motive. How else can we get our bearings? But to stop *permanently* is to falsify the characteristic Chaucerian complexity, to substitute a naive Arnoldian sublimity for the self-conscious, ever-shifting reestablishment of temporary stays against confusion which constitutes the true Chaucerian seriousness, a kind of biogrammar which finally proves so complex that it does not so much take over culture as become isomorphic with it.

Chapter 5
At and *Through:*
The Opaque Style
and Its Uses

When I was a graduate student writing a dissertation on the rhetorical language in Sir Philip Sidney's *Old Arcadia,* I came across a passage in one of Kenneth Burke's books which I found immensely heartening. It occurred in the midst of his discussion of "eloquence," early on in *Counter-Statement.* It was not a major Burkean pronouncement but merely one of those sidelong glances he always put in so that we who came after him would see that he had already thought through most of the ideas we would spend the rest of the century reinventing. This particular proleptic claim was about Lyly's mannered Elizabethan style in *Euphues.* "I sometimes wonder," Burke wrote, ". . . whether the 'artificial' speech of John Lyly might perhaps be 'truer' than the revelations of Dostoevsky. Certainly at its best, in its feeling for a statement which returns upon itself, which attempts the systole to a diastole, it *could* be much truer than Dostoevsky."* I was heartened because I felt that something like this was true of Sidney, too; that he was trying to glimpse a world where verbal ornament is as essential as essence, as serious as serious purpose, and as needful for man, and where ornament and essence, like systole and diastole, like breathing out and breathing in, constitute the life-giving oscillation of human life.

This paper offers a stylistic matrix which attempts to consider in *general* terms a subject—the uses of self-conscious rhetoric—which in so many *particular* cases energizes the greatest, and the most greatly disputed, Renaissance literary texts.

I am going to call such self-conscious rhetoric, in a generic singular, the Opaque Style. What we must first notice about the Opaque Style is that it works like a simple *At/Through* switch. Verbal patterns can vary in small increments, but our attention does not seem to. Either we notice an opaque style *as a style* (i.e., we look *at* it) or we do not (i.e., we look *through* it to a fictive reality beyond). We see either

* *Counter-Statement,* 2d ed. (Chicago, 1957), pp. 42–43.

a compulsive compound syntax or a weary Hemingway hero home from the wars. Our gaze snaps from one discrete attitude to another, as in those multistable illusions in which a vase becomes two facing profiles or an old crone changes into a young girl. The text itself does not change but we see it differently. How does such a sudden either/or self-conscious switch work in verbal styles? What patterns trigger it and why? Above all, how do you get from such *At/Through* simplicity to the complexity of literary response which it engenders?

The received wisdom on this matter has not, since Aristotle, gone out far or in deep. Transparent styles, because they work unnoticed, are good. The opaque ones, which invite stylistic self-consciousness, are bad. A style that attracts notice as a style turns every stylistic virtue into its corresponding vice, every sincere stylist into a decadent flaneur. Before you can get out of this dead end, you have to take the discussion out of its moralizing context and put it in a behavioral one. This is what I propose to do. When you construct a behavioral matrix, the following things happen: (1) you understand why the moral context prevailed for so long and what truths it points to; (2) you see what is wrong with our stylistic terminology in general and why; (3) you isolate the fundamental confusion endemic in Western rhetoric and poetic; (4) you begin to sketch an answer to the largest question which informs stylistic study, the role of ornament in human life. And, as a lagniappe, since I indulge myself in some analogues with painting, it may be a little easier to see how painting can be compared with poetry.

I

First, the *text*. Its instructions for the reader can vary from a simple behavioral trigger to a contemplation of the trigger for its own beauties. It can shout "Fire!" or invite us to become a fire buff, aim for a stock response or for free metaphoric play. We might picture a text spectrum as in part 1 of the diagram on page 68, with "Transparent" at the far left and "Opaque" at the far right.

The Transparent pole, at its extreme, would offer an unmistakable sign pointing to an unmistakable object or action: one word, one thing. Such an extreme aims to put us in touch with a reality standing by itself and in no need of verbal re-creation—simple mathematical notation, highway signs, directions for assembling your new sandbox, and the like. A little way in from this theoretical extreme would stand the C-B-S prose ideal, a text which has a style but conceals it, the universally praised style which does not show. This is not a transparent *extreme,* of course, since the "transparency" is created by artifice, by a style which *can be seen* if we look *at* it hard enough. At a further remove from this extreme we can locate the "clarity" which does show a little, but "shows well," as it were—the famous Drydenian clarity that is so often held up as the perfect prose style. The aim is always the substance of the argument, the scenery in the description, but one does stop occasionally for a "How well put!" or an "Exactly so!" without feeling that the author would flinch if he heard it.

The Opaque extreme would be, I suppose, those phrases of Homer which in Geometric Greek vase-paintings are used almost as a *visual* decoration, as patterns that made decorative as well as, or sometimes rather than, verbal sense. Calligraphy, too, would seem to fit here. A step in from this rigorous extreme would bring us to the frankly contrived opaque styles that run from Gorgias to Lyly to Joyce, and that we usually group under the term *kunstprosa.* Here, the style often becomes the meaning or, to put it another way, the style becomes frankly allegorical. Lyly's compulsive antithetical balance comes to shadow forth his hunger for emotional balance, and for a eulogistic covering of seeming judiciousness to mask the exhibitionism to which his frustrated ambition drove him. A step further toward the center and we come to the mannered styles—Browne, Johnson, Pater, Tom Wolfe—that are not frankly opaque and allegorical but still ask often enough to be noticed, even if only to establish clearly the persona of the writer.

In the middle, all the shades of gray. The middle here—just as with the Middle style as against the High and Low—is hard to define except in terms of the extremes. There are simply too many kinds of mixtures. Perhaps one observation should be made, though, about this muddled middle. Often when people talk of "clarity" as an artistic rather than a workaday, a "high" rather than a "low" ideal, they really are pointing to a style from the center, a mixture of the two extremes, rather than the pure transparency they think they are recommending. To put it another way, this kind of middle style can be "transparent" but to a complex, very serious and self-conscious kind of social reality.

How does a text throw the switch? Well, obviously, it can thicken or thin the ornament so much that we notice it. A sequence may be reordered, individual elements exaggerated or repeated, or the sequence broken off altogether. Or ornament can be ironically juxtaposed with plain speech, as when Henry V's "On, on, you noble English" finds an echo in Bardolph's "On, On, On, On, On." But a spectrum such as this implies a *gradient* of response. How do you get there from an *At/Through* switch? It happens, I think, by frequency of oscillation (see, too, pages 95–98 in "The Abusage of Usage"). Human behavior rarely offers examples of the pure extremes. A radically mixed state prevails. The frequency of oscillation from transparent to opaque increases toward the middle and diminishes at the ends. The right and left extremes offer only half of the *At* and *Through* oscillation, freeze the back-and-forth motion in an all *At* or an all *Through* phase. They aim for purity but pay the price of being static.

On such a spectrum, very different styles may, because they share the same frequency of oscillation, share the same position. A James making love to the period may bed down next to a Hemingway abjuring subordination as insufficiently tight-lipped. The uses and origins of language can be measured here too. If you agree with Cassirer that language primarily expresses not thoughts but feelings, then your center of gravity falls to the right. If, like a Freshman Composition teacher, you think pure exposition normative, you will stand balanced on one foot at the left and, as did the Paris critics with the Impressionists, direct morally outraged artillery fire at anyone on the opposite end who looks *at* words rather than *through* them. All the "ordinary language" skirmishes have been fought over this ground, as well as Plato's campaign for a left as against a right position, for "an abstract language of descriptive science to replace a concrete language of oral memory" (Eric Havelock, *A Preface to Plato*). The "subject" of the text will vary, too, more conceptual to the left; at the right, more about language itself. A neutral spectrum this, please note—no point morally superior to any other.

We can plot painting on this spectrum too, from representational to abstract. At the right extremity think of Mondrian and at the left a Dutch still-life bouquet of flowers, by Jan van Huijsum, say, complete with glistening dewdrop and horns-erect snail. Manet insisted that we look *at* not *through* a painting. This spectrum measures how much the picture invites *At* rather than *Through* vision. No point along its length outranks any other. You can, of course, generate a whole range of critical bickering by standing on one point and laughing at all the others. Thus Matisse, in the famous anecdote, when asked why his picture of a woman did not look like a woman, replied that it was not a woman but a picture. We all laugh with Matisse but he was as muddle-headed as his questioner, for the picture did invite a *Through* vision too, if only to rebuke it. I know of no stories like that about Mondrian, who could have made the joke in good conscience.

Such a spectrum seeks to plot not only representation but self-consciousness as well, the degree to which we are invited to consider paint as paint, words as words. On it can be plotted many, though not all, of the traditional nature-vs.-artifice arguments. The spectrum may seem embarrassingly simple, but failure to understand it has generated enormous confusion. The crucial question, though, is what role *we* play in triggering the *At/Through* switch. It would be easier if our response varied concomitantly with stylistic tumescence but, again, style seems rather to work like the neuron, to build up a chemistry unnoticed until it reaches a threshold which triggers the switch.

We need, clearly, another spectrum, one for the *perceiver,* in which the common reader shares the far left with *Through* and the critic as critic stands far right, with *At* (see part 2 of the diagram on page 68). We are talking about the perceiver, remember, not the perceived. A perceiver can choose to look *at* or *through* a painting or text regardless of what attitude the object itself suggests as appropriate. The simplest example of such willfulness, I suppose, is the Rorschach test. Or, like Mark Twain, we can look at the fiery Turner canvas and say that it looks like a tabby cat having a fit in a dish of scrambled eggs. At the opposite extreme stands the odd feeling critics often have when, after intense study of nonrepresentational art, they turn again to representation. Again, a neutral spectrum. No point morally superior, although, certainly, the aesthete will continue his quarrel with men who have met payrolls.

We can of course generate invidious comparisons, like C. S. Lewis's between the "Few" and the "Many," or Northrop Frye's between the critic as common reader and the critic as critic, or E. M. Forster's between "feeling a book" and "thinking a book," or Burke's between the "hysteric" and the "connoisseur." Here cluster all the critical arguments about willing suspension of disbelief, literature as therapy, Norman Holland's implacable exposure of how people really read, Morse Peckham's role-theory of art, and so on—all the ways in which patterns of attention vary a norm. And the aesthetics of photography fits here too—things are changed just by being photographed, as Andy Warhol tirelessly proved. Most critical theorizing about the text can without difficulty be translated onto this reader spectrum (the allegories—Christian, psychoanalytic, structuralist, Marxist—toward the left, formalism toward the right) and the critical conversation thus transfused with new life, or at least the old problems reworked in a different color chalk.

The same can be said for the third spectrum, which measures artistic motive and which lines up "Competitive," "Ethical," and "Dramatic" from left to right (see part 3 of the diagram on page 68). When you ask if Dalí is a "serious" painter, you are trying to place·him on this spectrum. In literature, some kinds of intentionality can be measured here, as well as endless theoretical disputes generated about such things as, for example, whether a detective thriller is literature or not. In discursive prose, this spectrum surfaces when you ask, "Is he really sincere?" We think, for example, that the Impressionist painters were serious indeed and their original critics thought just the opposite, but we are both thinking along this same range of measurement, arguing about motive.

When you think about it, such a spectrum measures human motivation generally. To describe the center, the normal vocabulary of motive stands ready, all the words for good and bad. But there is no proper vocabulary for either end of the spectrum, for competitive or for dramatic motive. Such motives are, though we use a moral vocabulary, not moral at all. We have no word for dramatic motive, loyalty to form, and so we press into service moral terms like "integrity" for an action that is not of itself moral or immoral. Nor is it aesthetic, properly speaking. It involves neither the connoisseur's detachment nor the critic's emotional distance. Just the opposite. It seems intimately related and necessary to the self, as Enobarbus finds after he has left Antony. I have used the word *honor* faute de mieux, as Jacob Burckhardt does in talking about the Renaissance, to indicate "that enigmatic mixture of conscience and egotism which often survives in the modern man after he has lost . . . faith, love, and hope."

Yet *conscience* is too moral a word, and *honor* in fact does duty all over the spectrum. We need a word that points to another range of behavior altogether. We seem to possess, like other primates, and perhaps other animals as well, a spontaneous urge to play, and to play with the forms of behavior as well as of matter. Such spontaneity may well bring with it adaptive advantage, but such advantage does not explain its essence. Bronowski, in one of his television talks, mentioned with puzzlement that Stone Age hand axes were often much sharper than they needed to be. That's the urge we need a term for. If it were not already morally tinged, we might use Kenneth Burke's term—*perfection.*

An odd cluster, then, at the right—art, or at least "serious" art; honor, at least of Burckhardt's Renaissance sort; games, or at least games played in the old-fashioned aristocratic, amateur way; mountain-climbing; scholarly research; the whole of purposeless purpose. It is the world of the man whom Burke describes in one of his "flowerishes" in the *Collected Poems*: "in a world full of problems, he sat doing puzzles."

At the left extreme, a more respectable group, the competitive and hierarchical urges that constitute our primate biogrammar. About how these urges (for status, pair-bonding, child-rearing, and the like) are wired into our biology, the students of animal behavior have taught us their revolutionary lesson. And for these urges, too, we have no suitable terminology. Ethics calls them pride as against humility, passion as against reason, but they seem the most reasonable and least individualistic thing about us. It is this kind of motive which, in romance, requires two knights to fight and see who is stronger before they can become friends. And in less romantic life it makes freeways, with their infinitely changing opportunities for triumph and display, so much more psychologically rewarding than buses. We clothe these primate urges in sober purpose—a Mercedes is after all a good investment—but nobody is fooled. Our sense of practical purpose is always squeezed from both ends of the spectrum and, when something has to give, practicality usually gives first. Competition can drive it to extinction and so can honor. And when the two extreme motives team up to constitute a sublimity, there is nothing we cannot do, whether build Chartres or put a golf cart on the moon.

If most people willingly starve for the O Altitudo! of their choice, there is nothing irrational about this sublime hunger. Such a potentiating combination of hierarchic and dramatic motive, game and play, may be our major conspecific feature, our dynamic center. At least, when a society tries to leave it out, to proscribe the motivational extremes in the name of practical purpose, it usually ends up destroying purpose. And if human motive is galvanized by the mixture of these two extremes, it is not hard to explain the ineffectuality of traditional ethics.

Where does the opaque stylist land on this spectrum? At both extremes. His originality lies in his uncompromising formal loyalty; yet, like John Lyly, he is not without hope that this high-minded independence will prove highly saleable. He wants to make a splash. On this spectrum, then, he is both completely *At* and completely *Through.* Faithful to the right extreme, he finds his ultimate truth in ornament. Faithful to the left extreme, he finds all truths to be but ornaments of power, intellectual history but a dance of the intellectuals. He thinks like Thrasymachus but at the same time sends Homo sapiens to the genetic cleaners as the great pastoral myths do, and builds his arguments on equality and love. It is no accident that pastoral and romance, the two genres built on these motivational extremes, so often use opaque styles. It may even be that we get from the one extreme to the other *by means of* the opaque styles.

I have shifted here from the poet's motive to our own to suggest how inevitable this movement is. Judgment about the artist's motive leads to judgment about his conception of human motive generally, and if we cannot agree with that conception, static is generated. It is this misunderstanding which funds the philosopher's quarrel with the rhetorician and our own with the opaque styles. We want to think that our behavior is purposefully motivated. We live for reasons and die for causes. The opaque stylist keeps suggesting instead the two reductive extremes. If in fact we simply act out a genetically imprinted biogrammar which equips us with our aggressive and submissive urges and our maternal, paternal, and other pieties, then philosophy is reduced to conceptual ornament, Benthamite eulogistic coverings. If, on the other hand, it is the spontaneous fountain of play which makes us bubble, then intellectual history is ornamental in another way, a genuine dance of the intellectuals.

Now when we judge behavior in the middle, we are always intuitively tasting for how much of each extreme went into the mix. Stylistic self-consciousness separates out again these extremes which we have carefully folded in, and such separation does not flatter our high-mindedness, an attribute we would prefer to keep fuzzily splendid in the Arnoldian manner. This spectrum of motive really measures, then, not what people say but how and why they mean what they say. It measures how we take ideas, how people use them. It measures how concepts are *embodied.* The embodiment changes everything. If you prefer your ideas disembodied, you will stand with Plato and the philosophers; if you think ideas, in their natural state, come in people, you will side with the rhetors. Since literary history has usually preferred its ideas disembodied, we can measure here its delight in discussing ideas in literature while ignoring how they are used. And, since this use is often conveyed through stylistic self-consciousness, literary history's remarkable tone-deafness to opaque styles no longer seems so remarkable.

From motive we move, again inevitably, to the reality that motive creates. Ever since William James, in the *Principles of Psychology,* reanimated the classic Western discussion of the *theatrum mundi,* social reality as drama, we have had at least one alternative to the self-sufficient positivist version. I am not going to summarize modern role-theory—the so-called *Homo duplex* thesis—but we might notice that much of it recapitulates the Western discussion of verbal styles. A whole branch of modern behavioral science has suggested that social reality is composed of opaque behavioral styles, that reality is radically and fundamentally theatrical, "sincerity" a special case of drama much as "clarity" is of verbal style. We find here the same radical inversion of play and purpose. In such a world Conor Cruise O'Brien can call the United Nations sacred drama, and a long series of social philosophers beginning with James and George Herbert Mead can depict the self as dramatic in growth, essence, and behavior.

Discussions of style, however, still assume a naive positivist reality. Yet for the opaque styles a dramatic reality obviously changes everything. Instead of being an artificial *imitation* of a positivist reality, they become the real-time re-creation of a dramatistic reality. A dramatic reality allows literature to break out of its critical solipsism and connect itself again to life. Wallace Stevens's dictum that "poetry is the subject of the poem" comes now to mean—if life can be "poetic"—that literature regains its contact with life, becomes statement as well as pseudo-statement, refers to something besides itself. The Platonic paradox dissolves and literature again shines golden, as Sidney knew it ought, built upon reality itself and not merely an imitation of it.

The modern expansion of animal behavior studies has reminded us of a third referential reality that we have always had available, the genetically imprinted world of the primate biogrammar, a world of impulses without a controlling self, the reasonless, conceptless world of dream and myth. Clearly, as I have already suggested, this world of opaque *behavior* is destined to revolutionize intellectual and literary history just as the *Homo duplex* thesis revolutionizes the Western discussion of style. To chart these changes, we need a *reality* spectrum, which will line up "Primate Biogrammar," "Ordinary Life," and "Drama" from left to right (see part 4 of the accompanying diagram). The variable measured here is individual self-consciousness. If we are imprisoned by basic compulsions, we live in an evolutionary past whose closest present analogues are myth and dream, worlds beyond sense and causality where things are hyperreal but we possess no sense of self. If we feel totally self-conscious, we put on the play-face (as they say of the chimps) at the other end. Both extremes suggest that our thinking of central purpose as static and homogeneous is wrong, that it is an unstable mixture of the two extremes, with purpose somehow trying to steer between them, and that in assuming static central purpose as referential, both rhetoric and poetic have gone methodically and seriously astray in both directions. Ordinary

1. TEXT	
Transparent	Opaque
(*behavioral trigger*)	(*symbolic trigger*)
(*stock response*)	(*metaphorical play*)
(*denotative clarity*)	(*stylistic excess*)

2. PERCEIVER	
Through	At
(*common reader*)	(*critic as critic*)

3. MOTIVE		
Competitive	Ethical	Dramatic
(*hierarchy*)	(*practical purpose*)	(*play*)
(*money*)		(*hobbies*)
(*game*)		(*honor*)
		(*form for its own sake*)

4. REALITY		
Primate biogrammer	Ordinary life	Drama
(*dream*)	(*central, "serious" self*)	(*ritual*)
(*myth*)		(*propaganda*)
		(*naive allegory*)

life is not just out there but is created and sustained in the middle by a struggle between the extremes.

At these extremes, we would seem to be both more determined than we usually think, and freer. The biogrammar imprisons us but the spirit of play frees us radically. And the freedom comes not, as ethics would have it, from dominating our pride but from ceasing to suppress our spontaneous sense of play. The *At/Through* metamorphosis seems specially absolute and self-reinforcing on this spectrum, as our passion for sincerity attests. This spectrum cradles us all on a dilemma's horns. When and why do we decide to look *through* rather than *at,* decide to credit a new reality rather than classify it as metaphor? Do we decide on a reality in order to identify the mimetic type or vice versa? (As Wilde insisted, it was not *painting* that was never the same after the Impressionists, but *London.*)

A number of traditional literary concerns assume a new aspect when this dramatic variable *is* reckoned in, from courtly love to Puritan hatred of the theatre, which makes perfect sense if the real fear is lest *life* prove theatrical. The moralizing terminology points to a real danger; this premise *does* undermine traditional morality, as we shall see. (And, under its lights, Wilde's paradoxes cease to be paradoxes. We can see him as developing arguments for a new kind of seriousness and a new kind of history.)

The lefthand, mythic extreme is as venerable as the *theatrum mundi* metaphor which complements it and has generated equal confusion— and for the same reason. How can we describe in ethical terms a range of motive logically and temporally prior to ethics? How decide whether it is a property of literature or of life? Is it only literature which varies here, or life as well?

II

My attempt to account for the opaque styles has now assembled four basic spectra of reference—Text, Perceiver, Motive, Reality—in a defining matrix. This matrix, depending upon its scale, is: (1) a model for the kinds of statements which define any literary or rhetorical term; (2) a model for theories of perception, visual or verbal, a map of critical misunderstandings, a schematic wiring diagram for the Tower of Babel; (3) a model for the place which opaque styles have in the scheme of things; (4) incidentally, a model for the ways in which painting and poetry can be meaningfully compared. The matrix is based on *a single variable*—degree of self-consciousness. Obviously, one can devise matrices built on different variables, or one can measure different phenomena, add different spectra. But they will not measure what is measured here: the various kinds of seriousness man has insisted upon, the various realities he has dwelt within. However incompletely detailed this particular chart may be, however insufficiently discerning in its emphases, we need one like it to account for the opaque styles. It answers the main question they pose—what do we mean by "seriousness"—and it does so without leading to an infinite regress. There are these *kinds of* position and no more.

We establish a seriousness by choosing one spectrum as fixed and referential and thus allowing the others to be measured and known. Sometimes we establish a referential constant without thinking about it, accept a reality just out there and interpret everything in terms of it, as Eric Auerbach did in *Mimesis,* or the Paris critics with Impressionist paintings. Sometimes a maximally self-conscious decision prevails, as when Bosch or Dalì, by the very hypertransparency of their painting, compel a totally reconstructed reality as referential. Most of the possible combinations seem to have been tried. Wilde's plays are, like Pre-Raphaelite art, a transparent imitation of a dramatic reality; Shake-speare's history plays are self-consciously dramatic imitations of a self-consciously dramatic reality, and thus become what they imitate, recreate it in real time; Lyly writes an opaque fiction about a dramatic reality, and so must settle for a less "realistic"—that is, a less identical and real-time—imitation. With the Greenwich Village production where an ordinary family was moved on stage to live their ordinary lives, the play was made maximally transparent to shock the audience into looking *at* the formal expectations it had been trained to look *through,* this by simply subtracting the expected form. The direct ancestor of this kind of drama is the "Evening" of the Italian Futurists, but less extreme forms obviously occurred much earlier. The clearest modern analogue in painting would perhaps be a work like Duane Hanson's "Self Portrait with Model," where he sits, depicted in pho-tographic realism, with a woman companion at a café table, reenacting a Polaroid shot from a Robbe-Grillet novel.

In these kinds of comparisons some odd similarities pop up. Dada, for example, expressed its intellectual nihilism or despair or bankruptcy by insisting that the only reality was the reality of abstract shapes. Every other reality had been contaminated beyond redemption; only shape and contiguity remained. Lyly and Nashe showed the same narrow faith, and in precisely the same way; the moral and conceptual apparatus had broken down and only the tropes and schemes remained. So, too, with Hemingway's compound style, I suppose. Or we might consider those allegorical interpretations of seventeenth-century Dutch genre painting in which homey scenes of homey life turn, their symbols read aright, into homey whorehouses. This combination of hypertransparency and opaque symbol is clearly the technique of Spenserian allegory also, and the two can be precisely compared. Or we can compare the Shakespearean pun, for example, with the broad and quick brushstrokes Frans Hals used in his later work to indicate hands or lacework; we see them in oscillation, both as brushstrokes and as lace.

Duchamp's "Readymades" (the famous urinal, for example) sought to trigger this same switch from *Through* to *At,* and here the Dada antecedents were equally clear. There was to be *no aesthetic ingredient.* Both Duchamp and Cage return to this point again and again. The "art" was all to come from the act of attention, the didactic emphasis on throwing the switch. Cage used a similar Dada technique in what some regard as his finest composition, a piece called *4′33″,* in which he comes on stage and sits at the piano in silence for that length of time and so creates the performance from the expectation and incipient meaning flowing from the audience onto the stage. In these instances, the observer spectrum forms the target, and so a meaningful comparison between music, visual art, and literature can be drawn.

An insistence on throwing the *At/Through* switch as the end of art does not begin with Dada, of course, but with Romanticism itself, as Morse Peckham has made clear in *Man's Rage for Chaos.* (It is quite possible to seek ancestors much further back, as I have done in *The Motives of Eloquence.*) Concern with throwing this switch on all four spectra becomes pervasive in Post-Modern painting and sculpture, and seemingly all the possible permutations have been speedily worked out there, from the hyperrealistic imitation of the physical world (Tschang-Yeul Kim's *Water Drops No. L1*) to Jean Tinguely's machines, some of which (*Rotazza 1*) simply invite us to look at machinery for pleasure rather than with an eye to purpose (this by subtracting all purpose and substituting play—here tossing balls out to the crowd); some of which allegorize the misuse of machinery (*Cenodoxus Isenheimer Flügelalter*) in the same way that Lyly allegorized antithesis; and some of which, like the machines that make an abstract drawing for you when you put a coin into the slot, imitate realistically (i.e., transparently) the production of opaque art.

Or we might remark the inevitable pattern of response to a work of art that aims to throw the *At/Through* switch only, *not* to provoke any aesthetic response. This is, of course, a trap. Throwing the switch *triggers* the aesthetic attitude. After doing that, the artist can retire and let the audience constitute his meanings for him and make him famous. This, in fact, is just what Duchamp did, and of course it worked splendidly. Most artists were not as uncompromising—or as clear-sighted about their own work—so that when they painted didactic pictures urging upon us the switch from *Through* to *At* vision, an aesthetic ingredient inevitably crept in. In Audrey Flack's painting *Shiva Blue*, for example, the subject of the painting is a jumble of tubes of paint. Point made: the means become ends, look *at* the paint rather than *through* it, paint noticed *as paint.* But the style that does this is transparent not opaque, and the result is a still life with a strong aesthetic ingredient. So, too, with Lichtenstein's comic-book paintings. The original didactic lesson is clear enough: stop and look at the painterly surface which you usually look through, accept simply as a narrative convention. But then, by scale-change and other more or less traditional painterly devices, he adds beauty to the lessons in perception. *Docere et delectare,* but by a new route.

There are plenty of modern examples of the Duchamp trap, inviting us to look *At* rather than *Through* and then giving us nothing to look at, especially in modern film, but the classic master of this allegorical trick is Rabelais. He is always inviting us to crank up the allegorical meaning-making machinery and then laughing at us for doing so.

Comparisons like these move in the opposite direction from the "music is frozen architecture" type, which try to talk about one art, metaphorically, in terms of another, try to convert space into time, or whatever. These are all doomed to inconsequentiality. If we say, to return to an earlier period, that Jan Steen is the Thomas Nashe of Dutch painting, we have not said much. But to argue that the tensions out of which Nashe builds his grotesque vision are all *At/Through* tensions and that Steen's, though his grotesqueries seem very like Nashe's, are built up through transparent means, reveals a real comparability.

Burke once remarked apropos theoretical disagreements that criticism should use all the information there is to use. The matrix suggests why this is never done, and why the critical enterprise so naturally becomes a bear garden of competing theories. Even if you want to use everything there is to use, you cannot use it all at the same time. The very nature of logical thought makes you want to take one spectrum, or one point on one spectrum, and interpret everything in terms of it. The rest of the chart is not totally ignored, of course, but is taken as a concomitant variable. A formalistic critic will concentrate on what can be said about the poem. He sets the boundary conditions of his discourse accordingly, and within them, if he has wrought with sufficient care and rigor, he ought to be unassailable. His study is primary because he has arranged the universe of his concern so that it must be so. Thus John M. Ellis, in the midst of arguing a role-theory version of formalism (in *The Theory of Literary Criticism: A Logical Analysis*), insists that questions of intentionality simply *do not exist* until a structure has been posited.

Within his own terms, Ellis is entirely correct. For the theorist who takes his stand on the observer spectrum, another set of rules prevails. He will not be, as Ellis is, upon thorns to decide what a poem is or is not, but he will have the same *kind* of problem. Will he embrace the whole spectrum or only one point on it? How will he conceive the literary observer, Frye's critic as critic, for example, or the numinous "Superreader"? Is the ideal reader to be identified by what he knows or by how he reads, looking *at* a style or *through* it? The problem of the ideal reader has been plagued by the same temptation that dogs the other spectra, the urge to reify the extremes, to place the ideal reader at one end or the other of the spectrum. Critical common sense suggests a place in the middle somewhere, but if you choose it, you may, like C. S. Lewis with his "Few" and his "Many," flounder in inconsistency. Yet if we had to choose between Frye's Critic as Critic, with his Frye-like encyclopaedic knowledge, and Lewis's insistence that the ideal reader means a balanced, mixed self, a fruitful oscillation between the suspension and the dominance of the ego, the matrix suggests that Lewis offers the more profound *kind* of explanation. A single consistent position, *any* single consistent position, leads to inconsistencies.

Ellis begins his intelligent and challenging study by attacking this critical pluralism. If we have learned to live with it, he argues, only laziness and lack of intellectual rigor have allowed us to do so. Pluralism leads to nasty in-fighting but no conceptual rigor, no definitive theory. But surely the nastiness and the search for conceptual rigor form part of the same process, the desire to fix one variable and derive the others from it. This does not lead to a hopeless and endless collection of critical theories. The matrix plots the boundaries within which theories can vary. An infinite number of theories there may be, but only a restricted number of types.

No single theory, it is clear, can be adequate in itself. It may proscribe part of the model, banish the reader or apotheosize him, but it will depend on the experience charted by the obelized part of the model even if, as usually happens, the proscribed element must be sneaked in by the back door. Every model of thought ought also to model the history of disagreements about that thought, and the two are clearly inseparable here. The matrix reveals how critical disagreements are generated and why they are so acrimonious. One is almost always being attacked not for an interpretation rendered within one's orientation but for that orientation itself. Nobody likes to feel the ground shake. The scholarly world might be more genteel could we agree that each theory, if adequately rigorous and comprehensive, creates the object it criticizes and so must be right—no need to argue. Different theories talk about different poems which happen to share identical *words*. Monet's "Impression: Sunrise" was a different painting, defined by a different structure of thinking, and referring as we have seen to a different reality, from the conceptual structure of the critic who used it in inventing a dyslogism, "Impressionism," to describe this new visual orientation.

Such conceptual rigor would indeed make us more peaceable, but the peace would not last long and neither would the rigor. For the rigor aims to be simple and reality is complex; the rigor allows things to happen consecutively, but in experience things happen all at once. The variables are being controlled in a sequence that itself is continuously changing. We will always continue to seek relief at the extremes, of course, because there life is simpler, and we often feel that, so long as it is simpler, we don't really care *in what way* it is simpler. Abolish mind, abolish body. Abolish gesture, abolish word. It doesn't matter which. Mankind wants only to reduce the variables—if possible, to eliminate them, outlaw chance. And the extremes are not only simpler but juicier. It is in their sentimental intensity that all absolutes are interchangeable.

I would argue, then, that the process of perception and of educated viewing and reading are complex in the same way. Theory tries to slow them down and clear them up, to simplify the lines of force. I am not knocking this endeavor. What else can we do? But we ought not to think we are describing more than we are or addressing the process itself rather than the rules formulated to help us see a part of it. And yet the process itself must exist, and it must be constantly varying, stopping one variable to register another and then reversing the order.

This amounts to saying that the *At/Through* switch operates between spectra as well as along each. It is the product of the continual horizontal and vertical variation that generates our sense of continuous reality. We might borrow here an analogy from human foveated vision, which can focus on only one area at a time. Consciousness, too, moves in a series of discontinuous saccades, momentary fixes of vision, and yet constitutes a seamless reality.

What we call "good taste" must be the skill we develop for this kind of perceptual activity. It is good taste that tells us to look at one surface and through another, look through a painting that requires it and yet hold the surface pattern in the eye. If we cannot both use a pattern and see it, then we can step up the oscillation between them to such a frequency that they seem one, just as a movie camera animates an image. We can now see why systematic critics have such trouble with value judgments. Value judgments express taste and depend, therefore, on intuitive fixings across the four spectra. Systematic critics adopt one spectrum as referential and thus, by virtue of their system, must dismiss value judgments. Taste and value cannot be described within any single theory, precisely because they mediate between the different theories. A systematic critic finds value located entirely in text, reader, or, as with Arnoldian high seriousness, subject, and thus methodically misses the point of value judgments.

I have been arguing that all critics are right, or at least more right, about the things they most bitterly and eloquently contest. This lesson has been taught by art history repeatedly since the critical outcry over the Impressionists. We show no signs of learning it, to be sure. We have learned instead that the funnier a contemporary painting strikes us, or the angrier it makes us, the more we are to look grave and mumble something about "tactile values." We have learned to worship humbug. This is not quite the lesson one would have hoped for. That all critical theories, like all poems or paintings, can be plotted on our chart does not mean, of course, that they are all equally significant or equally consistent in their own terms. But when we think how vastly silly we can all be as critics, it is reassuring to find such silliness part of how we respond to the world. What draws us in the other direction is that constant varying of our referential spectra at every fixing, that sixth sense for reality which every art tries to teach us.

I am not, I hope it is clear, arguing for a *critical* impressionism. Yet our tendency to talk about one spectrum in terms of the other is built into the way we perceive the world. It is the natural thing to do. We are always seeing and thinking of these variables in terms of one another and as long as we live in time will continue to do so. It is right of us to separate them and it is right, in an informed taste, to put them back together again. To chart how we differ shows both kinds of rightness.

III

The opaque styles, then, imply a reality, a self, a pattern of attention, and a range of motive different from those usually called "serious" but equally necessary to our own full reality. When put in a behavioral context they reverse the whole direction of thinking about style. The tail seems to have been wagging the dog all along. Art may be a special case of ornament and not vice versa, as Wolfflin suggested (in *Principles of Art History*) by calling art history "absolutely, primarily a history of decoration." And was this not what Burke was saying in *Counter-Statement* when he wrote that "Eloquence is simply the end of art, and is thus its essence"? Perhaps shelter is an *excuse* for architecture, not its cause, rhetorical display a necessary adaptive function that finds in communication its handiest occasion, interpretation an excuse to exercise signifying powers. This reversal of thought stands comparable to—and may be connected with—that reversed flow which converted the eighteenth-century argument from design into the Darwinian argument for natural selection. As with the opaque styles, the data remain the same but a different gaze changes their significance totally. The rabbit becomes a duck. Style, instead of creating the decorative surface of reality, may be reality's major constituent element.

The pattern of reversals implied is fundamental. United with role theory and the dramatic genesis of the self suggested by Mead, Piaget, and others, it suggests that we sometimes behave as we do for the hell of it, or rather for the reality of it, to maintain reality. Perhaps, like other primates, we need signal-exchange in the same way we need vitamins, behave "honorably" to sustain the self, and contrive our purpose and moral struggles to intensify our drama. Art is life carried on by other means and more intensely. If so, the whole body of thought which tries to save our souls by improving our communications seems pointless. We will not avoid misunderstandings through improved communications. We need our misunderstandings and will tinker with our language, if need be, to enhance them. This view would seem also to condemn all those theories of art which argue for release-of-tension and order as the end of art. Yet purposive expectation holds so firm a grip on how we think that it seems to provide the ground of our being. Our theory of motive is built upon it. People do things for *real reasons*—food on the table, a roof over their heads, an enemy trounced. Our morality—people are independent accountable selves—depends on it. Purposes can be codified, some allowed and others proscribed. Our theory of history depends on it too. The historian must build his account of the past on the premise that people do things for what we are accustomed to call "real reasons." A historian may be literary or deterministic, but the reality he describes can not.

A similar reversal—though it would not be germane here to spell it out—is implied by the opposite reality, the human biogrammar. Man as an unselfconscious primate role-player provides the logical complement to the *Homo duplex* thesis of man as social plus central, dramatic plus purposeful self. These three sources of motive and types of reality together constitute the complex Western reality we find it so hard to describe.

If reality is constructed in this way, communication and its logical correlate, purpose, must have arisen as products of the interacting extremes rather than vice versa. Practical purpose must be a secondary activity emerging from the primary evolutionary pressures of the biogrammar on the one hand and play on the other. It follows that a discussion of style which holds this kind of purpose as referential for man will misconstrue not *one* fundamental source of human motive but *both* of them, and hence badly misunderstand the mixed reality in between. This is what has happened in the West since Aristotle.

Our rhetorical and critical terminology for style has multiplied with such fecundity, I think, because it has tried to keep faith with a felt reality more complex than its theory has ever allowed for. Our terms leap from spectrum to spectrum because they want, like taste, to span all levels, to chart reality completely. If this fecundity is not wholly satisfactory, at least it argues a kind of wisdom, a desire to see reality whole. And when the full range of each spectrum is plotted, and as a variable is related to the others, the endemic metaphoricality of our terms seems more explicable, too.

Obviously I cannot deal with this explanation in detail here. Let me instead suggest a few examples from criticism and rhetoric.

Take a term like *realism.* Each spectrum seems to cherish a central term like this, indispensable and totally vague, which refers elastically to whatever point on the spectrum we choose to applaud. Once we see how this elasticity works, "realism" works too. Why not applaud whatever we want to? So with "sincerity" for the motive spectrum, "clarity" for the text, and so on. The trope/scheme distinction, too, resolves itself: trope and scheme coincide if the style is opaque, diverge if transparent. The different senses of the high-middle-low division of style now obviously refer to one of the four spectra. The metaphor-simile distinction is explained: if we are talking about the world, it is a simile; if about our perception of the world, a metaphor. An oxymoron generates its paradox by yoking two spectra together: "O Heavy Lightness" couples a lightness which refers to the event with a heaviness which refers to the beholder; "cold fire," "sick health," "bright smoke"—they all work this way. Some rhetorical terms obviously refer to the text alone, some to the speaker, some to the reality imitated. Virtue changes to vice if the style stands to the right but the observer to the left. Move the observer to the right and you get the terms of irony. Puns, too, seem more comprehensible. They get better the more intensely they yoke *At* and *Through* vision in a single word.

Defining according to the matrix seems to clarify not only basic terms but also why they have been so hard to clarify. Defining them is like pressing a drop of mercury on a pane of glass: press down on one spectrum and the terms glide away onto another. They must be defined by one another and we can only chart how. The critical debates about the meaning of literary decorum, for example, make more sense if we relate the style spectrum to the reality spectrum. For an opaque style, decorum is automatic: you adjust your reality to fit the style and not, as with Horatian decorum, vice versa. But, of course, the reality measured against varies too, and here, historically, the fun has begun.

To distinguish among kinds of reality may shed light on what Aristotle meant when he said that poetry, more philosophic and serious than history, yields general truths, not history's simple particulars. Might these patterns of inevitability characterize dramatic rather than positivist reality? Is it in a dramatic reality that things are likely? Aristotle defines a general truth as the kind of thing a certain kind of man will do or say either probably or necessarily. Aren't we dealing here with a reality conceived dramatically? If so, the fundamental confusing circularity in the *Poetics* opens up, a circularity responsible for eons of muddled mimesis. Aristotle is forever changing the kind of referential reality he uses without realizing, or of course telling us, that he is doing so. Aristotelian universals are really the world seen from the stylistic point of view. Universals are not certain kinds of statements about reality but rather statements about a certain kind of reality. A good deal could also be done in this regard with negative concepts like "suspension of disbelief" and "negative capability." By restating them in positive, opaque rather than negatively transparent terms, they become states not when you

have to deny one kind of reality but when you are *affirming* another
kind. It is easy to see, in this connection, how the various arguments
for literary and stylistic "purity" are generated. They simply vary our
basic tendency to plead to a spectrum's extremes. Conceptual rigor
inevitably moves us in that direction.

Within a definitional matrix, the form/content dichotomy falls away,
too. Form and content are discrete at the Transparent end of the text
spectrum and homogenized at the other. Or, as we have seen, we
can choose to *see* one way or the other. Behavior itself can be purposive—and so means and end will be separate—or self-pleasing,
existing for its own sake, homogenized. Yes, style *is* meaning, when
by "meaning" you mean stylistic reality, instinctual reassurance and
rehearsal. No, style is *not* meaning, when you mean concepts. The
form/content distinction is just like the life/art one, and varies in the
same way.

We can glimpse, here, a way out of the paradox faced by theories
of poetry which insist that poetry is simultaneously possessed of its
own special truth and yet is based on metaphor. If poetry possesses
its own kind of truth, if we must accept it as a separate reality,
suspend our disbelief, look *at* rather than *through,* then we are in
trouble if we posit the centrality of metaphor too. For *At* vision
dismisses the referential reality which creates the metaphor. Suspending
your disbelief annihilates metaphor. To preserve metaphor means *not*
suspending your disbelief, keeping a reality you can compare things
to. You cannot argue for a theory that does both unless you are
willing to allow both to happen, in oscillation, one after the other.
This is so obviously what actually occurs that the fundamental inconsistency has scarcely been noticed.

The terms for literary genre seem to make more sense, too, when
plotted on the matrix. Sometimes genres are distinguished on the
text spectrum, sometimes on the *reality* spectrum, and often the two
are confused. We use genre distinctions when we assume that the
world is all one thing and categorize the ways to imitate it. But when
we assume that all *literature* is homogeneous, then the genre categories
simply become different kinds of life, categories of reality. Romance,
for example, may become the aspect of life that most reflects rhetorical

motive, as in *Cymbeline*. It seems an easy distinction to make but nobody makes it.

A complete taxonomy of genres based on all four spectra seems possible. It may even be possible to read horizontally instead of vertically and thus to explain, in terms of our polar extremes, why genres like to come in pairs, tragedy and comedy, pastoral and romance, primary and secondary epic, satire and apocalypse, and the like. Aristotle again provides the earliest example of generic confusion, tragedy and comedy being defined sometimes as types of drama and sometimes as types of self. To work out genre theory spectrum by spectrum seems more promising. Take tragedy, comedy, and satire. If we plot them on the reality spectrum, tragedy clearly maximizes the central self and explores the consequences of doing that. Comedy maximizes the social self and explores the consequences of that. Satire seems to set the one point against the other, to juxtapose two different ranges of motives, moral and dramatic.

Let me develop this point about satire to show the kind of thing that can be done.

It is not simple excess, nor simple sin, which the satirist pursues, but a particular kind of behavior. In the name of plain and sensible purpose, he reproaches motives that are dramatistic, behavior that is ornamental. The *vir bonus,* the plainspoken man, is the man not given to such symbolic, stylistic behavior. For him the referent realities are not dogmatic but pragmatic; man's basic purposes, not the psychic superstructures we love to build atop them, constitute his fundamental reality. He never forgets that pompous buildings once were things of use. He never lets us forget it either.

Now such a stance simplifies human motive considerably. The satirist would have us think his division isomorphic with good and evil, appearance and reality, but this is obviously applesauce. Man's role-playing self is as real as his central self and not necessarily less virtuous. And the same goes for society, considered as drama and as positivist reality really "out there." The satiric simplification, though it comes as a stinging lash, hides a compliment. If man does not often act from plain purpose he *should,* and this implies that it is natural for him to do so. Edenically, he is a being of naive purpose.

He has a central identity and creates a substantial society. This is Egg. Chicken is his *dogmata,* all his dramatic feints and agonies, his sentimentalities, his affectations. We are serious fellows, at least to begin with, and the satirist flatters us by assuming so. He bestows an Eleatic being on us, as it were, in passing. Maybe this is why we like satire.

Orthodox satire thus deprives man of the stylistic communion by which he creates a society and makes himself welcome and understood in it. It denies that imposture has *any* place in human behavior. It is always taking man out of the complex setting which makes his behavior intelligible, if not rational, and plunking it in a context of plain purpose where it seems quite mad. In this new context, of course, we can enjoy the madness more.

In addition to the satiric interface, the reality spectrum suggests an answer to the related but much larger question of literature's relation to morality. Inasmuch as literature depicts the dramatic self and society, it will teach us something about dramatic motive. It will suggest a range of motive neither moral nor immoral, a range of behavior that sustains the self in society. The lesson thus taught will be intimately related to how we behave, and so in a sense morally useful, but it will not emerge from dogmatic morality. Dogmatic morality is externally imposed; dramatic motive comes from within us, formed by the process that creates the self. If the two never meld they forever masquerade as each other, and one of literature's principal businesses is to follow these tergiversations. The act of following is made that much easier because style is an *At/Through* code like morality, and so one can always be made to stand in for another. Yet literature cannot make us "better," if by that we mean more likely to follow a specific moral code. It may well make us worse, because it suggests a range of motive wholly outside moral bonds. We can commit villainy for the pure dramatic pleasure of it, like Iago, and so place teaching and delight in direct opposition.

Most discussions of literature's relation to life think backwards. They search for the dogmatic ingredient in literature rather than the stylistic ingredient in life. The Marxist who wants literature to sponsor revolution would do better to think revolution a proper dramatic illusion which literature teaches him to stage. The relationship of literature to politics, in fact, focuses the major moral force of "literariness." Literature teaches by teaching new roles, and to the extent that we alter our conduct not by minute increments but by discrete leaps, basic changes of role, moral reform will proceed by literary means. Curiously enough, the closer we get to purely *religious* reform, to being "born again" as we say, the closer we come to the purely literary, dramatic process: total role change. Something magically discontinuous inheres in this process, as Shakespeare, to his commentators' puzzlement, so often insists. The sudden state change reminds us of the sudden transformation of words when we look at them self-consciously. It reveals the same *kind* of multistable illusion. If the mechanism of moral reform is dramatic transformation, then about this mechanism, presumably, literature has everything to teach.

Literature's teaching delights because it can infuse the moral range of motive with formal pleasure. The good guys–bad guys polarity we so enjoy may be not an ethical necessity but a dramatic necessity to which we fit an ethical mask. Conventional morality takes advantage of this dramatic force, "slipstreams" it as they say in auto racing, and so we think of it as inevitably moral. It is the opposite. The slipstreaming allows us to *enjoy* moral struggle. It thus supplies the real defining category of "catharsis," a suggestively meiostic term Aristotle applied to an enjoyment which, within his conception of reality and of human character, ought not to exist at all.

Ethics must always—this is its founding premise—describe behavior out of context. The very existence of literature constitutes a protest against the inadequacy of the conventional ethical categories for the full range of human motive. Because literature's particular subject is exactly this mixture of motives, it must contradict its commentators— always zealous to purify it, to explain it by *either* a moral theory *or* a formal one—who either formalize its morality or moralize its ornament, homogenizing its oscillation into that embalming breath students feel on their necks when they mutter about murdering to dissect. The radical discontinuity between moral and formal theories of art would seem to be simply the basic *At/Through* stylistic decision writ large. And so the opaque styles, whenever they return in force, signify not decadence but its opposite. They show a life and vigor in the oscillation that constitutes reality.

IV

I have been saying that the opaque styles, seen in a behavioral context, stimulate us to redefine our critical terminology and, in the process, resolve some critical perplexities. They make whole and comprehensible the Western discussion of style, so that it ceases to work against itself. Both rhetoric and poetic are freed to confront human communication in its complexities. If the model works for life as well as literature, as I have argued, then versions of the same model ought to have appeared in the behavioral sciences. I think they have.

Perhaps I need not mention the computer analogy itself, except to suggest that the *At/Through* switch may open verbal style to computer digital analysis in a new way. And it is scarcely less obvious to mention the other ways in which rhetoric's traditional concerns have been newly treated by other disciplines. Role-theory and dramatism have mapped the right end of the reality spectrum and sleep research is busy on the left; game-theory is mapping the left end of the motive spectrum and numerous play studies aim at the right; anthropologists like Clifford Geertz are talking of cultures as texts; and perception psychologists have revolutionized the relationship between seeing and knowing. (Perhaps we can see, too, an analogous development in economics. The Mundell-Laffer hypothesis argues for a conception of the world economy as a closed set of variables like the literary matrix I have just discussed.) Edward O. Wilson, in *Sociobiology*, has suggested that we should "biologicize" ethics, and this seems to imply a rethinking of the left end of the motive spectrum in much the same way that I have suggested a rethinking of the right. The two together ought to produce a new terminology for ethics. And, at a higher level of magnification, Ernest Hartmann's research (as reported in *The Functions of Sleep*) has suggested, in the action of the catecholamines, a neurochemical basis for self-consciousness. If, as he contends, D-state sleep, in bypassing them, omits the serious self, then he has found the plus-minus neurochemistry of motive.

These various levels of magnification have not been considered together, to be sure. That would be too raffishly interdisciplinary. Yet the convergence should hearten us. It suggests an answer to the last question posed by the opaque styles. Why did they develop? What survival value do they possess for man? What good are they? Classical humanism rightly understood (that is, the way I understand it) would answer that they make man whole. They insure that both his natures, social and individual, are sustained in that creative oscillation which has galvanized Western culture. They prevent him from falling into a simplistic high seriousness, whether Aristotelian or Arnoldian. They also—a longer-range function—act to brake his overwhelming purposiveness, prevent it, as Gregory Bateson has argued, from flowing suicidally strong. They set up a cybernetic circuit which deflates our sublimities and returns them to play.

The opaque styles are finally, then, protective of man. They can be triggered by all kinds of repetition or discontinuity. An author is likely to trigger them when he wants to render us self-conscious about his motives—either purely formal or purely purposive—or about our motives, our insatiable appetite for significance, our tendency always to look through a text to our own reality beyond it. The opaque styles are likely to insist on their own opacity, their own meaning as styles, to suggest a dramatic rather than a positivist reality and a role-playing rather than a central self. They can act, on the level of words, as role-playing does on the level of behavior to stimulate innovation by recombination. Such styles are triggered when, for whatever reason, a literary text or a culture wishes to control its purposiveness, to emphasize the way its knowledge is embodied in people. The opaque styles will be used, that is, when a society needs to renew its reality, intensify exchange between the two polarities of its being. Multistable illusion, in such a world, stands at the center of human adaptability.

In a longer evolutionary view, this adaptability probably came about to ritualize or displace aggression, as the biogrammar's counterstatement to it. Opaque styles work to return us to play. The characteristics of an opaque style which I began by describing, for example—reordering, exaggeration, repetition, and discontinuity—I found in just that form in a summary of research on play in the higher primates. It may be that self-consciousness, as indicated in so many human activities by the *At/Through* multistable choice, arose in order to effect just this displacement. If so, the rhetorical figures, in their grand Ciceronian occurrences, must model this ritualizing displacement of aggression, must be pure play. And the switch itself must be the controlling, enabling device for morality. "The artificial speech of John Lyly" may indeed be "'truer' than the revelations of Dostoevsky." Or, if not truer, at least as true, the "breathing out" which complements an equally necessary "breathing in."

Chapter 6
The Abusage of Usage*

The distinguished philosopher Brand Blanshard, once musing in a *Yale Alumni Magazine* on the pleasures of being an emeritus, put down as the first of these the freedom from reading student papers. "Though I enjoyed both lecturing and discussion, reading student papers was another matter. It is the grimmest part of a teacher's life." He went on to discuss the desperate stratagems which he, like most of us, embraced in order to do his duty and yet save time and sanity—checklists of standard errors, rubber stamps, the lot. The most desperate of these, of course, has always been to write a book, a book which will put down, clearly and economically, all the things one must say over and over about student papers. Then the office hour, purified of repetitive detail, will become more efficient and more refined. One can say simply, "Look, take this book and read it, memorize it in fact, rewrite the paper, and then come in again if you have any further questions."

Jacques Barzun, toward the end of a long career which has always included an interest in prose style as well as a distinguished practice of it, has finally written the book, *Simple and Direct: A Rhetoric for Writers*. It is difficult for such books, by their nature as textbooks, to be more original than the errors they seek to chronicle and prevent. Thus Barzun, under such snappily traditional rubrics as "Tone and Tune, or What Impression Will It Make?" and "Composition, or How Does It Hang Together?" offers the same advice American composition

* This essay was originally published in *The Virginia Quarterly Review* in 1977 as an essay-review of Jacques Barzun's *Simple and Direct* and *The Harper Dictionary of Contemporary Usage*. Although it differs somewhat in format and address from the other essays in this book, I have included it because the conception of literacy it discusses is precisely the one the other essays seek to change. The reasons for my disagreements with the books under review will be much clearer, I trust, in light of the other essays than I was able to make them in the review itself. The confused mixture of C-B-S prose theory and social snobbery which both books reveal still supplies the dominant American conception of literacy, and this muddled and impoverished conception has had widespread consequences for the teaching of writing in America. Robert Pattison has made just this point in a brilliant new book, *On Literacy* (Oxford University Press, 1982), which anyone interested in these issues must consult.

texts have been retailing for the last seventy-five years. The purpose is "to be understood aright"; the prose is to be "simple and direct"; and for the writer, "the first requisite is sincerity." The proper "tone" (by which Barzun seems to mean "style") is a "plain" and "even" one, as exemplified, we are told, by both Whitman and Mark Twain. Neologisms are all but outlawed: "New words are rarely needed outside trade and technology." If genuinely needed, better Anglo-Saxon than Greek or Latin derivatives: "Think how much plainer and finer, less obtruding and conceited the tone of prose would be if from the beginning we had said speed meter and not speedometer, laundry shop and not laundromat, moving stairs, icebox, and lift, instead of elevator, escalator and refrigerator." "Gas station" and "scotch tape" show "the true democratic spirit" but not "discotheque" or "polyester." The "wooly metaphorical style" of our generation is to be banished by "Principle 16": "Worship no images and question the validity of all." And jargons—in fact, all fancy wordings—are proscribed.

Barzun's standard advice on organization ranges from "Grasp the subject and do not let go" to "move forward without wobble and meander." Variety is to be shunned if it threatens "sincerity and truth." We are to subordinate intelligently, use the active words, keep related elements together, keep parallel elements parallel, and take thoughtful notes. As for closing, "finality is of course still in order. Nobody wants to stop, but rather to end." There are exercises after each section, collections and mistakes headed by rubrics like, "This exercise should not prove difficult—the faults exhibited are obvious. Record your distaste and rewrite." And there are half a dozen intercalated passages of specimen prose (Sayers, Hoffer, Sapir), called "Time Out for Good Reading," followed by reflections and questions. *Simple and Direct* is, then, the mixture as before, aimed here at an advanced undergraduate and graduate student audience.

Mr. Barzun's book, Clifton Fadiman's dust-jacket puff claims, is both funny and "alert to every manifestation of our linguistic barbarism." I have enjoyed Barzun's wit over the years as much as the next man, but I don't see it often here. He aims to be clever but he ends up more often than not sounding schoolmarmish: "Those who are tempted to fiddle and tinker with words and who thereby lead some users astray might bear in mind that making up words is an art, not merely a trick of combining roots according to rule. ... Nowadays innovators carelessly stretch meaning as well as coin new words." Such admonitory fingers waving on every page make the reader feel preached at.

As for being "alert to every manifestation of our linguistic barbarism," Fadiman is surely right. None—not even the panelists of the *Harper Dictionary of Contemporary Usage*—can stand before Barzun. Much of his book is in fact a discursive usage dictionary, an extended castigation of all the slovenly mistakes, seemingly, which have annoyed him over a long and busy career. "Hopefully" and "contact" figure strongly, of course, as well as advertising clichés and bureaucratic mumble-speak—the standard list of villains. Most literate people, one would guess, enjoy these Fowler games, but they must be played with a light touch. Barzun takes such mistakes, and especially his own impatience over them, with supreme seriousness. "Of particular annoyance to me," which prefaces his annihilation of "personal," might be the title of his book. If often he is sensible, sometimes he is shrill or silly: "economy size (a *large,* not a small quantity); belabor (beat with a stick, not 'make a to-do about,' which is *labor* a point)"; "'Assistant Town Clerk Mary Jones was married yesterday at noon to piccolo-player L. C. Robinson.' This is the tone of bureaucratic regimentation." Sometimes he seems almost to court annoyance. In one exercise, for example, we find, "for the billing [and cooing!] month of June the charge will be 7.2% higher." Cannot a billing month differ from a calendar one, as a fiscal year from a calendar one? The great thing in Fowler games is to sound like Fowler and not like those pedants who, as Barzun himself says, "stickle over minor points" but "stay blind to the significant ones."

The *Harper Dictionary of Contemporary Usage* might accurately be described, perhaps, as Advanced Fowler Games. If you enjoy growing livid, with a carefully selected group of friends, over a misused "hopefully," over "author" or "gift" as a verb, over "disinterested" for "uninterested," over whatever current solecism happens to jiggle your bag of spleen, then you will doubly enjoy the *Harper Dictionary*, for there you will find your exasperation echoed by a panel of distinguished experts, all crying, "Ugh," "Loathsome," "Butchery," "Horrible,"

"Awkward," "God," "God, no," "Incredible," "Abominable," "Highly objectionable," "Ye Gods," and "!!!".

Two things, besides this periodically invoked chorus, seem to distinguish this new usage dictionary from the fuller and more scholarly ones (I read it against Evans and Evans, *A Dictionary of American Usage*; Partridge, *Usage and Abusage*; and Fowler, revised and unrevised): it includes more very recent usages (Watergate talk, New York police slang, computerese), and it takes pains to include a number of Briticisms. It betrays, in fact, its origins in the newspaper column of its editors, "Words, Wit and Wisdom," and the files of oddities such columns inevitably accumulate. Those addicted to Fowler games, or who need to know the British word for "popsicle," will want to add it to their library. Those interested only in a basic reference text ought to choose one of the fuller and better ones.

II

Both these books share not only the same superior tone but the same unexamined premises, and tone and premises together make for a humorless and finally an unintelligent conception of language. Both Barzun and the Harper panelists seem to think that we live in a time of special linguistic barbarism and that their job is to stave it off. They think of themselves, that is, as academicians, and their job as preserving civilization by preserving its language. Now there is no convincing evidence for any of these flattering, if also disturbing, prejudices. Usage has always changed, and the change has always been regretted, but civilization has not seemed to rise and fall in concomitant variation. Newspeak is nothing new. Ideologies all distort language in about the same way. The language of the Henrician revolution, say, with its Troynovant myth, was no less violent in its distortions than the master-race language of Nazi Germany; it just seems so to us because we applaud the one and loathe the other. England in her eclipse seems no less well-spoken than she was in her greatness. People who say "ain't" or who use "hopefully" in the same way they would use "however" are not necessarily the moral inferiors of those who do not.

One would think such platitudes need not be rehearsed, if these books and many like them did not so resolutely construe their task in moral terms. The only question to be asked of language usage is "Right or Wrong." (Maybe this is why the chorus of praise and damnation from the Harper panelists so recalls in its vehemence the language of religious disputation.) This moral premise distorts every question asked in its name. It is not that the good/bad distinction is not useful. It is. But if it insists on being the only possible distinction, it will be much less useful than it could be if it were recognized as but one kind of question among many which usage poses. The good/bad distinction, in isolation, dooms itself, as these two books illustrate, to sterile repetition and finally to working against precisely the kind of correctness they seek to recommend.

The most obvious distortion introduced by this moral polarity is the conception of linguistic change it reveals. Although some among the Harper panelists fudge a bit, they generally assume that change is bad. Changes are mostly mistakes, and the main motive for mistakes is ignorance. This assumption outlaws the *play* of language as a principle of change, of development and discovery. Consider, for example, one of the usages that drive the Harper panelists into fibrillation, the use of "author" as a verb: "He authored three books in a single year." "Why," Frank Sullivan asks, "use 'author' when there's a perfectly good word—'write.'" Why indeed? None of the panelists seems to have pondered the question, yet the fact that it can be asked disproves a major premise of these two books, that changes in usage are usually *mistakes*. No one could claim here that a native speaker would not *know* that "write" was an alternative. Whatever motive substituted "authored" for "wrote"—boredom, play, a desire to emphasize the act of writing as a role—it was not *ignorance.*

The "usage-abusage" cast of mind is willing to admit such play only if, as Anthony Burgess says in condemning "author," some new nuance of meaning is added. That is, play is permitted only if it is properly purposeful. Yet Burgess is a student of Joyce. He knows that play must be free, purpose*less,* if it is to keep language alive. He knows that language, even—maybe especially—ordinary language, is at least as playful as it is purposeful and expressive. Forcing all changes of expression into the good/evil polarity guarantees that most of ordinary language—the main concern of usage dictionaries, one would think—will be not only misunderstood but systematically misunderstood. One might, in fact, profitably and properly think of usage dictionaries as condemnatory histories of verbal play.

Communicating concepts is the least of human purposes, most of the time. Communicating attitudes is far more important, and just playing with words, staving off boredom, perhaps equally so. Slang will perpetually renew itself just because we *need* to play with words, to enjoy them. Jargons will always coalesce not only because we need specialized languages but because we enjoy private ones, and because we enjoy metaphor. Jargons collect metaphors which express our attitude toward what we do, our sense that it is a separate kind of activity, with its own roles and characteristic identity. They allow us to declare our membership in a group and our participation in its values. (They are thus, in fact, instruments of *clarity,* in that they proclaim the *context* in which an assertion is to be understood.) The moralistic attitude toward usage cannot understand this range of expressivity. It can only condemn. Such play, it is argued, stands superfluous to the real, true, and only purpose of language: to express thought clearly. And yet such playful superfluities generate the main changes that any discussion of changing usage must take into account. Oddly enough, the point is made, and precisely, by one of the authors Barzun quotes for his style, Eric Hoffer:

> We are more ready to strive and work for superfluities than for necessities. People who are clear-sighted, undeluded, and soberminded will not go on working once their reasonable needs are satisfied. A society that refuses to strive for superfluities is likely to end up lacking in necessities. The readiness to work springs from trivial, questionable motives. . . . A vigorous society is a society made up of people who set their hearts on toys, and who would work harder for superfluities than for necessities. The selfrighteous moralists decry such a society, yet it is well to keep in mind that both children and artists need luxuries more than they need necessities.

It is the love of ornament, of play, that keeps language interesting and us interested in it. The great, fertile, inventive ages of language have always been ages of intense ornamentation or, like our own, ages of the persistent metaphoricality that Barzun so deplores. This whole range of expressivity—nine-tenths of language, one is tempted to say—the good/bad polarity ignores by definition. It looks at "Thanks much" or "splanch" (new to me, too: a wonderful real-estate shorthand for "split-level ranch," which, of course, sets the Harper editors yowling) and can only unlimber the admonitory finger. Thus the really significant questions never even get asked. The first thing that strikes one about the Watergate/White House talk—deplorable by definition, of course, because a jargon—is its metaphoricality. Why did they all feel the need for such language? Why all those homey reductive metaphors? What hungers did they feed? Such expressiveness is condemned in the name of clarity, of course, but read aright, isn't such language likely to tell us more *clearly* about the motives of those villains than a neutral expository prose ever would? A time always comes in studying language, and it should come early, when you credit the linguistic surface. You assume its total expressivity. That is the way you really learn from it. If you insist on translating it into denotative prose, you will never understand it. You will be exactly like the man who, though he knows—and deplores—that some people say *perro*, or *chien*, or *cane*, or *canis*, or *Hund*, also knows that God's real name for a dog is *dog*.

III

In the moralistic analysis of style, virtue equals clarity, and sin is obscurity. Neither the Harper panelists nor Barzun has given this equation another thought. It is what Kenneth Burke calls a "god-term." Yet a moment's reflection will demonstrate that clarity is a disjunctive category. It points to a coincidence of attitudes, measures mutual contentment. It does not refer to any necessary verbal ingredients. How can it when there are obviously an infinite number of ways to be clear? And when the things one wishes to be clear about are so often feelings about, attitudes toward, a subject, rather than the subject itself? "Clarity" is a subset of the larger category "Satisfaction," and satisfaction can come in many ways.

Failures to be clear are, much more often than not, successes rather than failures. They succeed in expressing very clearly a muddled state of mind, or in making perfectly clear a whole cluster of attitudes surrounding a conceptual message. What is usually called lack of clarity is often rather the presence of something else, something the virtue/vice polarity cannot account for and thus registers as a pure negative.

The fundamental premise of both these books, of the whole usage-abusage orchestration (admonitory finger for "orchestration"), is that mistakes in usage cause misunderstandings. Most of the time this is simply not true. The context usually makes things clear. In fact, it is only because the context *does* usually make things clear that the solecism stands out so. If, 19 times out of 20, we did not see that, though the speaker said "disinterested" he meant "uninterested," we wouldn't heat our minds so about it. A real misunderstanding would occur. But it rarely does. Instead, a solecism occurs. And, though the Harper panel would have us think all culture stands at hazard, solecisms in language don't make any more—or any less—difference than any other mistake in manners. Look, for example, at "disinterested" and "uninterested." The reason for the confusion seems plain. On the pattern of "disinclined," "disengaged," "disenchanted," people assume that the "dis-" works the same way with "interested." For their sins they get this torpedo from Anthony Burgess: "The diminution of meanings is what Orwell's Newspeak is about." But is it really a diminution? Children learn quite young that there is more than one word for an object. Language ensures itself against misunderstandings not only by context but by synonym. It doubly overdetermines. If dis- and un-interested fall together, we will still have "unbiased," "impartial," "neutral," and many more. If we stand in danger of running out of synonyms, the same process of metaphorical invention that Barzun and the panelists so dislike will make up some more. We are not going to run out of words.

As for such errors being Newspeak, this is the old "foot-in-the-door" ploy used at all levels of argument—most notably in our time to justify the American presence in Vietnam. Once your explaining machinery is reduced to such an on/off simplification, you guarantee yourself simple-minded explanations for linguistic change. People make analogies; they get tired of one rhythm and, as in "Thanks much," invent another; they invent a new word to make the night-shift go faster or to sell a product or to hide a fear. Or, like the woman writing to the Welfare Department, they get harried and write, "Please acknowledge that I have given birth to twins in the enclosed return envelope." Surely they are not all sinners, collaborators in a vast Newspeak conspiracy which only the Harper panelists can prevent. Clarity, if in one way the end of language, is also the end in another way, the death of language. Change and error and chance and play grow up intertwined. There are none of these in the "usage" view of language; and there is no fun, and no generosity either.

The worship of clarity as the only laudable aim or result of prose amounts really to a leftover positivist prejudice. It assumes that language is totally referential, than an independently existing object "out there" is matched by a single word for it "in here," an assumption, one would have thought, that had been declared dead in other areas of thought for a couple of generations. It is, in America, a variation of what C. Wright Mills might have called "crackpot practicality," the conviction that words are only tools for the practical life, the pliers and screwdrivers of communication. The best prose style is the wholly transparent one, the world seen undisturbed by our attitudes toward it. Now, aside from the troublesome fact that such neutral perception has for a long time been proved impossible, such an ideal draws a number of difficulties in its wake. It is hard to teach and to learn what, it being transparent, you cannot see. Barzun is right in insisting that "a person who wants to write adequately must put his mind on words to the point of self-consciousness." Words must indeed, as he says, "become objects in themselves." It was precisely because they appreciated this home truth that the classical rhetoricians approached language and language pedagogy through what was finally a theory of ornament, a continuing detailed discussion of the figures of speech. Play, ornament, imitation, these, they saw, led to that acute self-consciousness about language which permits the student to go beyond the rules and continue his stylistic education on his own.

Barzun's pedagogy, and that of what we might perhaps call the Harper harpies, leads in precisely the opposite direction. They would argue ornament and play, the poetry of language, out of existence. Barzun's book and the attitude toward style which it represents thus work against the very purposes he would embrace. "Words, in short, must be *there,* not unseen and unheard," he argues, and then follows a book in which prose style is made simple, direct, transparent— unseen and unheard. Of course he does not really teach style this way, because he cannot. He offers what he considers examples of the transparent style in his "times out for good reading," but these work against his purpose, as do all such sample collections of "good modern prose styles." What Barzun really teaches by is his lists of errors. You can see errors. Errors are the *substance* of his book, as they are of the *Harper Dictionary.* The moralistic dichotomy prevents them both from seeing "error" as a subcategory of ornament, of the attitudinizing, poeticizing, evaluating use of language, and hence, in a very fundamental way, prohibits them from seeing what they are really doing. We begin to touch here on the settled and fundamental unintelligence of both these books. Both Barzun and the Harper worthies are interested in language for its own sake. They like to play games with it, to talk about it, to look *at* it rather than *through* it. Yet they are all prisoners of a theory of prose style which insists that the good style is looked *through* not *at,* that the good style is the unornamented, unmetaphorical, unslangy, uninventive style that never shows. They thus argue against their own real benefits and practices.

It might be possible, in fact, to argue that the theory of normative clarity as the end-all of prose style is responsible for the blindness to language which the theory of normative clarity seeks to remedy. The theory may *cause* the problem rather than cure it.

To argue thus is not quite the same thing as to argue for obscurity, to insist that in language "anything goes." To argue thus is again to fall into the moralistic dichotomy as the only frame of reference possible for language. No, the first requirement would seem to be to chart where "clarity" really does fit in the whole spectrum of linguistic communication. It is, like strictly disinterested honesty, a special case in human behavior and must be seen as such. It is a form of satire finally, an exposure of motive by the stripping away of attitude. Clarity is finally as artificial as La Rochefoucauld's *Maximes,* and for the same reasons. Perhaps this is why people so reliably flee it. It is too piercing and too simple. People don't think of the world neutrally, without attitudes. The attitudes will always flood in. If we want to think straight, about prose or anything else, we must understand such attitudes, not abolish them.

A mature and sensible theory of clarity, when it comes, will, I think, chart a process which oscillates between looking *at* the surface and looking *through* it. The frequency of oscillation is fast in "good," "clear" prose. In fact, I think the real variable for value judgments lies just here—the faster the oscillation, the better the prose. This conception of clarity would seem to make sense of the world in just the way that science does, for do we not now think of science as this kind of oscillation, at a considerably lower frequency to be sure, between hypothesizing on the one hand and testing on the other? The disproof of the theory of normative prose style, that is, would seem to follow Karl Popper's disproof of induction. We never approach the world without a conditioning premise. Our mind, to use Popper's metaphor, is a searchlight, not a bucket.

Popper does not argue that theories should not be tested but only that we should see what theories are, how they work, and should realize what the limits of testing are. So would I agree here. Conceptual thought obviously requires a different kind of language from poetry, but it is not a fundamentally different one. The frequency of oscillation is just different. Unless you understand how that oscillation works, unless you see "clarity" as only one point on a spectrum, you will never understand even clarity, much less written language. The mechanisms of expression, like those of perception, are constant, form a continuum; they do not divide into complementary extremes. By insisting on clarity as the only value in prose style, the usage guardians blind themselves to the real nature of clarity, as well as to everything else. Academicians represent a genuine part of the process of communication and the theory of style. But only a part. They stand to stylistics as the metaphysicians do to philosophy. Their job is, by setting language against itself, to refine and make consistent the set of symbols. Their job, that is—a nice paradox—is essentially *non-*

referential. They are not really talking about clarity or communication at all. Their real job is to make language consistent with itself. And, of course, this can only be done through verbal play.

IV

Any genuinely *referential* theory of meaning, of style, must deal with attitudes primarily, because human behavior is stylized, is primarily attitudinized. Usage thinking, armed with its reductive satiric premise, takes much the same place in a general theory of style that satire as a genre does in literary theory. It is a simplification but a needful one. It aims at the methodical exposure of imposture, realizing all the time that such exposure, and the theory of "real" motive on which it depends, is itself yet another pose. Good usage is, in fact, about as likely to save the world as satire, and for the same reasons. Both premise, as paradise, a world of plain-dealing, of total honesty with ourselves and others. The best satirists have always realized that theirs was an idyllic vision, and a hopelessly *impractical* one here below. The "usage" people, still imprisoned in their crackpot practicality, cannot see so far. They still pretend that their vision of pure and untrammeled rational communication is the only genuine, honest, true, efficient, and practical vision. The Harper panelists cannot be such ninnies in real life—we know they are not—but in the *Dictionary* they are prisoners of their own simplistic theory of prose style. They advocate a theory of style which, had they really practiced it, would have insured that no one would ask them to serve on panels.

It is clear, if we think about it for a moment, that the application of clarity to the prose of the past denatures it. The usual standard of comparison used to be Dryden. (Barzun's seems to be Abraham Lincoln, an example even more malapropos, if that is possible, than Dryden.) But it really always has been a preposterous assertion that the vast richness of English prose from Malory onward yielded only Dryden's clarity as its flower. What is not so clear is how clarity as a god-term denatures the *present* as well as the past, systematically disequips us to see, and enjoy, the richness around us now. Kenneth Burke's apothegm, that every way of seeing is also a way of not seeing, has never found a better application.

The persona of the satirist has been a good deal investigated by critics. All agree that for satire the satirist's pose as *vir bonus* is crucial. So for these two books. How we read them depends on how appealing and convincing we find the presented persona. Persona has always been a problem in usage dictionaries. Fowler has been worshipped— and rightly so, to my mind—because he is such a delightful satirist. We read him as we do Horace. For this reason, Fowler's Fowler will always be the volume of choice for connoisseurs. Gowers is a schoolmaster. Fowler was a satirist.

It is perhaps already apparent that I do not think the personae of these two books, the one individual and the other collective, come off especially well. The first thing that strikes me, as I have tried to point out, is that they work at cross-purposes to themselves, illustrate what they seek to disprove, create what they wish to abolish. Or, to put it in "Simple and Direct," they don't know what they're doing. Their conception of human behavior—and this is disastrous for a satirist—is ludicrously simple-minded. It is a commonplace commentary on satire, but a true one, that the satirist must in some way cherish the vices he castigates. The more Juvenalian and violent he is, the more must this be true. He must, like Juvenal, obviously *enjoy* laying about him, but he must also—and here Juvenal is unsurpassed—let us know that he lays about him partly just because he *does* so enjoy it. He himself is in his way as self-serving as those to whom he applies the lash.

It is here that both these books fail. They believe in their own virtue. As we have seen, what they really consider, nine times out of ten, is a matter of taste, not of communication. The great solecisms all start out, or shortly become, largely a matter of social snobbery, of "U" or "non-U" as the British, always more candid than we about their delight in snobbery, have it. What the panelists object to is not failure to communicate. They object to ignorance, laziness, above all to people who really do share the utilitarian attitude toward language which the panelists recommend but so markedly fail to embody. They dislike people who do not care about language for its own sake. So, let me hasten to add, do I. But I don't see that my dislike of them makes them any worse, or me any more virtuous, at least to begin with. Nor do I think that the American people's utilitarian attitude toward language—"Let it work is all I ask"—necessarily means the end of the world. If you are going to be a language snob, you ought to realize that that is what you are and not pose as the Defender of Public Linguistic Virtue. You ought not to enlist, in the name of reason and good sense, all the irrational attitudes toward language which you affect to deplore.

V

Snobbery, one of the Harper editors informs us, "does not belong in our democratic society." Therefore, to savor its pleasures, we must disguise them as virtues. This is what the Harper panel and its editors proceed to do. They enjoy all the pleasures of outraged taste and of outraged virtue at the same time. Make no mistake about those solecisms. They love them. One panelist has a sign on her door prohibiting entry to anyone who misuses "hopefully." You can scarcely enjoy your friends' mistakes more egregiously than that.

This pose is not a specially attractive one. The panelists think of themselves as Tom Jones but they come across as Blifil. One keeps murmuring to oneself, "Because thou art virtuous. . . ." "Snob," the *Harper Dictionary* tells us, means "one who acts smugly superior to others." Fowler games, at one end of the spectrum, are pure snobbery; at the other, genuine acts of self-reflection about the state of the language. The *Harper Dictionary* is a snob book from start to finish. It objects, in the name of communication, clarity, and civilization, to what really offends it on the grounds of taste. And it makes the worst mistake a snob can make. Although the panelists try hard, very hard, to be witty, they end up sounding boorish, silly, and repetitive.

Sometimes they are plainly ignorant as well. Take, for example, the use of *gift* as a verb. A cento from the panelists: "Dreadful," "Vulgar advertising jargon. NO, NO, NO," "No, No," "Ugh," "No! No! No!," "Loathsome," "Highly objectionable," "I hate it," "Horrible," "Awkward," "God," "Horrible," "God, no," "It disgusts me." This is the genuine language of snobbery. But what about *gift* as a verb? It has an interesting history, it turns out, as the *OED* reports it. It has been used as a verb since the beginning of the seventeenth century. The citations include a lovely line from a seventeenth-century sermon: "If God have not gifted us for it, he hath not called us to it." The verb seems to have been used right through the nineteenth century. Yet when it surfaces again, it evokes the yahoo chorus I have just cited. Why? The current usage as a verb comes from advertising, and advertising, for the person of letters, is the big enchilada, the main villain. However genuine a villain advertising is (it probably, by its play with language, does as much good as harm), what we have here is guilt by association, a snobbish verdict masquerading—ignorantly—as linguistic virtue. If we use *gift* as a verb, we will make the same kind of mistake newcomers used to make in Louis XIV's Versailles when they knocked on people's doors ("Horrible," "Awkward," "Loathsome") instead of, as all sensible and knowing people did, scratching at the door with a fingernail grown long especially for this purpose.

Two of the basic questions that never seem to get asked about usage dictionaries is who uses them and for what purpose. Are we to picture a beginning or frequent writer who wants to use *accessorize* as a verb but will not if the *Harper Dictionary* forbids it? There may be some such, but surely they are not the typical cases. These people will go ahead and do as they like. They are doing the work of the world, and they'll use the word that comes to hand. They will be like the man who does not know he is misspelling a word and so is not tempted to look it up. They lack, as we say, an "ear" for language, and it is the ear, finally, that tells us the difference between "disinterested" and "uninterested." How do you cultivate an "ear"? Barzun knows the answer as well as the Harper panelists—wide reading. You cannot memorize rules, you will not even want to try, until you have an intuitive knowledge of language, until you have cultivated some taste. Now usage dictionaries, if you browse through them, can help you confirm and sharpen your taste, but they are unlikely to awaken it. They move, again, in the opposite direction, argue that intuitive judgments are not intuitive but conceptual, codify them, render them a matter of rules. They would keep us perpetually on our "p's and q's," and a love for language does not lie that way. The perpetual single focus on correctness kills enjoyment, makes prose style into one long Sunday school. Usage dictionaries, that is, can teach us only what we already know. They tend to be the affectation of—well, of people specially interested in usage. They are most useful as the central document in a continuing word-game played by sophisticated people.

We face in America, there is no doubt about it, a genuine and genuinely frightening crisis in literacy. But the illiterate students who crowd the schools and campuses do not make the kinds of mistakes that vex Barzun and the Harper people. The mistakes of the new illiterates (admonitory finger) are much less trendy and far more fundamental. The needful pedagogy is as yet unclear, but it will certainly, when it coheres, stand far from the sin-and-redemption simplicities offered by the books under review. For we finally ask of the usage-and-abusage doctrine what we finally ask of the preacher—why haven't you been more successful? Why have so many, many books, all saying the same thing, failed so dismally to improve the situation? If what is really needed is the habit of wide reading before such advice can work, have we not said that we must be literate before instruction in literacy can do much good? Browsing in a usage dictionary is great fun, but for the wrong reasons. Knowing that *debag* is the British schoolboy's slang for taking someone's pants off, or that *argy-bargy* can mean a vociferous quarrel, will not save the world or solve the literacy problem. These words are just fun to know. And the same is true of watching Jacques Barzun, when he *is* funny, playing the *vir bonus* of language.

What will the answerable pedagogy be like for our time? Well, we can say for certain that it cannot be, as the usage-dictionary philosophy of language is, built on a pattern of fundamental misunderstanding about the nature of language. No successful pedagogy can. And, while the old pedagogy has failed for many reasons, clearly one of them is that its fundamental principles are wrong. It has mistaken a bandaid for the science of medicine. It has been a boomerang pedagogy, exacerbating the problem it sought to cure. At present so many social and political influences distort and mask the effect of these theoretical misunderstandings that it may seem unimportant to clear them up. Not so. The *fons et origo* of our problem is that instruction in language is based, when it is based on anything except the teacher's desire to get through the hour unharmed, on mistaken positivist premises which have been disproved in other areas of thought for a hundred years. You can neither understand nor teach a subject by making special cases—and purely denotative clarity is a very special case—into norms. There is finally no substitute for knowing the real boundary conditions of your subject. You need not be *against* bandaids (I am *for* them, and have dispensed my share) to argue that they offer no proper substitute for the study of medicine.

VI

Barzun is certainly correct that we must learn to see words as words, cultivate an acute self-consciousness about them. But the way to do that is to study words, the whole spectrum of prose styles from the most ornamental to the least, and study them all as possible strategies for different attitudes, places, and times. Put aside the moralistic polarity and study how, in fact, style works in the world, relates to and molds human behavior. Study styles, not preach about and at them. Any pedagogy that hopes to work must educate intuitive judgments, not try to avoid them or legislate about them. We are good, finally, partly by intuition. It is the same with prose. What we need here, as in the curriculum in general, is to move from concept to intuition and back, from poetic knowing to scientific, the movement Whitehead recommended so long ago in *The Aims of Education*. He called these two phases the stage of romance and the stage of generalization. Instruction in prose style has embraced both, but it refuses to put them into oscillation. There is plenty of pure romance—it is called "creative writing" usually, and its pedagogy is, as Terry Southern immortally put it, "Right out of the old guts onto the goddam paper." And there is the usage-abusage doctrine, which is all integration, all rules. The new pedagogy must combine both, and set them to work in the study of verbal style across its whole range. There is no reason at all why we snobs cannot go on playing Fowler games. If, however, they are mistaken for a serious, intelligent, and comprehensive pedagogy of style, then something has gone badly wrong and they are likely to cause more misunderstanding than they are worth.

The problem, at heart, is really the relation of formal to moral theories of art. I have been suggesting, of course, a poetic pedagogy for style, a pedagogy to complement—and indeed to surround, since it is so much more important—the older prescriptive theories. We cannot really notice words unless we love them, and love of words means the study of poetry. And it is in the relation of moral and formal theories of poetry that the root of our misunderstanding lies. I cannot here spell out how this relationship ought to be understood (I have tried to do this in the other essays in this book, especially in chapters 5 and 8), but perhaps I can offer at least an apothegm: since human behavior is so fundamentally stylized, language will reflect behavior most accurately when *it* is stylized; the study of style is practical in the most *immediate* way, in that it explores the stylistic and intuitive sources of our basic human motives. If you do not understand this, you will, as do these two books, fundamentally misunderstand how language does in fact mislead. And if you look for the causes of misunderstanding so steadily in the wrong place you will never see them in the right one.

The premise of the *Harper Dictionary*, and Barzun's premise too, is that the literate man is surrounded by an ocean of ignorance. This is, to be sure, the satirist's perennial pose, but which of us does not feel it keenly just now? Yet ordinary people, every day, make the most acute stylistic judgments in other areas of their life, show the must acute stylistic sensitivities. Is it that they *cannot* be made equally aware of language, that it invokes a range of stylistic judgment other areas of life do not? I think not. The great question is how to tap, and then train, that great reservoir of stylistic expertise. To do it, you must first understand the stylistic roots of behavior. Teaching and Delighting always return to one another in poetry because they find their common ground in verbal pattern and behavior, both matters of style and in the same way.

The final weakness, then, of these two books lies in their misunderstanding not of prose only but of behavior. Their conception of motive is, like their conception of style, grotesquely simplistic. We speak either to be clear, or to deceive. Good or bad. Rational or the reverse. The great compensatory spectrum of motive is the one that stands right outside this polarity—the spectrum of play. Once we allow it in our universe of discourse, the fruitful pedagogical oscillation that Whitehead counsels comes into being almost by itself. Barzun and the Harper panel will cease to talk at cross-purposes to themselves, to reenact a playful attitude while counseling a moral one. They may even, confronted with the problem in its fullness, see that their moral indignation is essentially playful, that they feel indignant in order that they may savor fully the pleasures of indignation, that this behavior disproves their counsel, that the attention to language they recommend leads to the stylistic play, the very endless free variation which they abhor.

These two books, then, are not remarkable for their freshness of thought or the innovation of their form. They are both, as I have said, the mixture as before. But they are none the less interesting for that. For if they do not offer a new genre and a new pedagogy, they demonstrate beyond a doubt the bankruptcy of the old, and for this we ought to be thankful. In this matter, they are equally eloquent. I have long admired Barzun's work and his career. In his combination of scholar, teacher, and dean, where are we to find his equal? Yet when he imprisons himself in an outmoded form and adopts its simplistic axioms of clarity, brevity, and sincerity, look at the humorless result. What he has done is illustrate the intellectual bankruptcy of the ethical mode of stylistic analysis. When Barzun says, in his introduction, that "Rhetoric in its essence is not concerned with your reason for writing," he goes fundamentally wrong and stays there. The disastrous premise permits nothing else. Likewise (admonitory finger) with the Harper panelists. People of great distinction in many kinds of endeavor, people possessed of savvy, sense, and determination, men and women of the world, when they are fed questions based on fundamentally incompatible and misguided premises, turn into a collection of silly snobs who mistake their preoccupation with verbal scrimshaw for the cause of civilization. The fault lies in the axioms of the genre. Perhaps people will always talk about language in moral terms, since it is so much more enjoyable that way, but we ought not to elaborate this practice into a pedagogy. We are not talking here about, as Johnson put it, the "few wild blunders, and risible absurdities, from which no work of such multiplicity was ever free." We are talking about the fundamental axioms of the inquiry.

Any serious usage dictionary of the future ought to chart usages, not condemn them. It should tell you that if you use *gift* as a verb you will have the New York literary establishment down on your head like a thousand bricks, but it need not smugly confuse the falling bricks with the preservation of culture. A genuinely new usage dictionary would understand, and show that it understood, how language is really used in human behavior. It would try to explain *why* the usages it discusses changed in the way they did. It would outgrow the whole Newtonian interlude that has given thinking about style a positivist bias since the days of Dryden. It would see that clarity is a very weak and incomplete god-term, and it would substitute for it a spectrum covering the whole range of prose styles, from the most transparent to the most self-consciously ornamental. And it would not come on, either as single spy or in a battalion, as the guardian of virtue.

It would have been a gratifying task to report that these two books, coming from such impeccable sources, really did any of these things, really had anything new to say. Alas, they do not. They simply combine, scarcely even in a new dress, the same old gossip, snobbery, good sense, good taste, misunderstood premises, and sanctimonious self-satisfaction which in the last hundred years have passed for thinking on the subject of prose style.

Chapter 7
Should English Departments Take an Interest in Teaching Composition?

"Bombs educate vigorously," Henry Adams maintained. Population bombs, apparently, don't have the same effect. Although several have hit English studies in the last twenty years, we seem to have learned very little. First, the baby boom that followed World War II prompted us to assume that what goes up will never come down. After that bubble burst, a series of social and demographic changes brought more black and Hispanic and, in California, Asian-American students into our teaching lives, but this fundamental change has prompted no fresh thinking that I can detect. And now have come the current waves of immigration that are bringing more first-generation Spanish-speaking students, more first-generation Asian immigrants speaking a dozen languages, more Middle Eastern students, and so on. With these new bombs bursting in air, the American system of public education has broken down, and the fifty-hour television week has stepped in to fill the void. To gift-wrap such alarms and excursions, the world during these twenty years has become, through revolutions in trade, energy, and communications, a genuinely global society. European culture has ceased to be the defining focus for Western thought and, yet more important for English studies, England has ceased to be the defining focus for America's connection with Europe. Finally, during these years, what promises to be the biggest bomb of all sneaked up on us—the computer revolution. The written and the read word have suffered, in their whole manner of existence, a radical electronic transmogrification.

English studies, meanwhile, has matured the disciplinary focus begun with the foundation of the Oxford English School in 1894. The critics and the philologists, after a long period of guerrilla warfare, stand more or less at peace, *aequo Marte;* the discipline has divided itself into specializations by period, genre, and great figure; it has developed bibliographical procedures which allow it to treat English texts with biblical scrupulosity; and, most important, it has developed a critical philosophy which sanctifies its departmental and disciplinary status. The argument that literature constitutes a reality apart from ordinary reality, deserving of study in and for itself, was present from the first, though for a long time it was exemplified by only a very few scholars (most notably Ernest de Selincourt in England and Thomas Lounsbury in America). The argument came into its own with the New Criticism, of course, and later with the work of Northrop Frye and others. And, although the "privilege" of literary discourse has now come into question, it is fair to say that faith in a "literary" truth distinct from scientific truth is what still legitimates literature as a subject to be studied for its own sake.

This process of disciplinary growth has now reached full self-conscious maturity: practitioners in the field are introspecting on the boundary conditions of their own activity, anatomizing it into its careerist, gamelike, and creative aspects. The maturation was accelerated by the two go-go decades of academic prosperity from 1955 to 1975, a flood of students and money that released English studies not only from composition instruction, until then its historic base in America, but also from routine instruction in the lower division. The discipline was thus freed to draw in upon itself, become graduate- and professional-centered, and sponsor metalevel reflections upon literary texts and critical inquiry—that is, reflections upon itself.

These years brought an impressive improvement in the quality and sophistication of literary training. Many bright people came into the profession and suffused it with their wit and ambition. Although occasionally diverted for a moment by the social explosions of those years, for the most part the discipline matured in a self-enclosed way. Self-enclosure was, after all, its enfranchising assumption. And this concentrated attention produced not only a *blumenzeit* of literary criticism but a concomitant maturity in bibliographical and linguistic and philological inquiry as well. No knowledgeable person would want to belittle, or to damage, this powerful maturity in the discipline. But, as we are now finding out, such maturity presumed a specific social base—the reigning society of 1894, in fact, when the Oxford English School was founded: white, literate, and at least middle class. English studies now provides a superb instrument to educate such a society. The society in which English studies in America must function, however, is no longer predominantly middle and upper middle class, nor is the dwindling white segment of it any longer reliably literate. English studies, like so many armies in the past, now stands superbly equipped to fight the previous war.

Meanwhile, as this disciplinary Maginot Line was being brought to its full perfection, there was poor old English Comp. Composition was everything that English studies had striven for a hundred years not to be. Avowedly a "service department," it had no room of its own in either theory or practice. The very opposite of self-enclosed, it served as time and circumstance dictated. Freshman writing, technical writing, business writing, legal writing—you name it and composition people would try to do it. Because the teaching loads and strains were desperately high, nobody went into composition who didn't have to or stayed any longer than forced to. These unwilling instructors might not have much theory, but they did know what their students were like. They were not fooled by the 1960s' genial fantasy of "the best-educated generation in American history." They knew a big problem was coming and was going to last a long time.

Now it has come, and composition is prospering—even getting a room of its own—and English studies wonders what it should think and do about it.

We have, on the one hand, a powerfully mature discipline and its concomitant career-game, with a sharply dwindling demand for its services, as it chooses to define them. On the other hand, we have an enormous social need for instruction in language, a need that will continue, whether enrollments in English pick up or not, for at least a generation. Can we bring these two worlds together? Use the talents and methods of English studies to address the literacy crisis? Conversely, use the literacy crisis to support English studies through lean times, preserve this discipline it has taken a century to define? Opinions differ. At one end of the spectrum stand the old guard in literary studies. They will have nothing to do with composition—that is the old "service department" routine: fix up the secondary schools and let them do it; it is not the university's business. At the opposite extreme stand the composition conservatives who want nothing to do with literature. They can be old veterans who resent the incursion of the "literati" into their status-poor but sometimes well-paying turf; they can be new-minted theorists who want to reinvent for composition the theory which literary criticism has spent the last hundred years working out. Both groups want to follow the route literary studies began in 1894. They want a room, a department of their own.

In mid-spectrum lurk a few puzzled folk trying to answer a question that can be asked in two different ways:

1. What is the relationship between teaching literature and teaching composition?
2. Should English departments take an interest in teaching composition?

Literature people characteristically formulate the question in the first way, composition people in the second. The first way looks inward to theory; the second outward to the pressures of an "insistent present."

To the first question, about the relationship between teaching literature and teaching composition, the history of twentieth-century English studies suggests an answer. That history chronicles the search for a literary theory which would legitimate English studies as an independent discipline. The resulting theory argued that literature should constitute an independent inquiry because its pseudo-statements present an independent order of truth. This legitimating departmental premise has surfaced in several guises since its synthesis from Renaissance golden poetics and its rebirth in Coleridgian thinking.

If this theory is true, or assumed to be, no English department can bear an intrinsic relation to composition teaching. However the latter may go about its business, it deals with communication in the "real" world—"out there." It deals with nonprivileged texts, with "prose" rather than "poetry." To define literature as privileged by implication defines composition in an opposite way. Composition becomes the study of communication in a world that is posited as the very opposite of literature's "imaginative reality." What I have been referring to in this book as the C-B-S theory of prose style follows understandably from such an assumption.

In such a polarized orchestration English departments will occupy themselves with the visionary moral order that literature is thought to present. The Composition Section will teach an "effective communication" tailored to context. This division of labor represents pretty much where we are now—*or at least where we think we are.*

For if this conception of literature is incomplete and misguided, then the state of affairs it implies can never fully come about. Literature can never absent itself from the "real" world nor composition do without literature and literary criticism.

So let's sketch out the opposite case, bearing in mind some points already made in chapters 4 and 5. Let us suppose that literature does not constitute a separate reality, but that life itself is full of "literary" elements. We might picture the relation of "literature" to "life" as a spectrum. At one end of the spectrum stands neutral "real life," detached from man and his recreative imagination. At the other end, that recreative imagination stands by itself, detached from flesh-and-blood reality, a world of fantasy.

Pure "Life" _____Pure "Literature"
            Social Roles   Ritual   Drama   Fantasy

But there are all kinds of mixed states in the middle. Most of what we call reality, in this way of understanding the problem, is "literary" to one degree or another.

We might also, looking at our case from the point of view of the perceiver rather than the perceived, remember the *At/Through* spectrum constructed in chapter 5 (p. 68, above). At the *Through* extreme, we are never self-conscious about the act of seeing or reading; we read only "for information." At the other extreme, we read or see only for style, look *at* a visual or verbal surface rather than *through* it. On neither spectrum is "literature" all one kind of experience and "life" all another. And the extremes on each spectrum are asymptotic; no pure cases exist. In this orchestration, literature does not stand apart from "reality"; it constitutes and suffuses it, much as role-playing constitutes social reality.

If this conception of literature be accepted, it brings along with it a different conception of self and of social reality, as so much of contemporary sociology and cultural anthropology makes clear. And it changes how we think about composition. The C-B-S theory now covers only a restricted range of prose composition. A resolute insistence on transparent prose gives way to a symbiotic exchange in which a prose surface both creates the reality beneath and is in turn affected by it. I have argued this case in *Style: An Anti-Textbook* and need not repeat it here. But the main point must be made: in this alternative conception of literature and of composition *the problematic relationship between the two simply disappears.* They represent different points on the same series of spectra. There is no difference *in kind* between them. Teaching literature and teaching composition form different parts of the same activity.

English departments, then, find themselves trapped in a paradox. To preserve their discipline they may have to interest themselves in composition. But if they do, they must discard their legitimating premise as a separate field of inquiry.

What, now, if we ask our basic question in its practical form: "Should English departments take an interest in teaching composition?" For many departments, to be sure, this question no longer makes sense. They may not be *interested in* composition but they have *become* departments of composition. For them teaching literature performs, statistically if not emotionally, a secondary function. The meaningful questions for them are: "Can we learn to like what we have to do anyway?" "How can we harmonize these two endeavors?" But there are departments which don't face this *argumentum ad baculum,* this ineluctable circumstance. Not many, but some. For them, the question occurs in its pure form: "Is there any reason why English departments should be interested in composition if they don't have to be?"

What answer can we give? Well, first, admit candidly that some compelling reasons suggest they *should not* take an interest in the problem. The theoretical paradox just examined, for one: an interest in composition threatens the English department's legitimating premise. Practical problems threaten as well. Teaching literature, for most who do it, proves self-renewing. It is no mere cliché that one returns from teaching and reading Chaucer or Shakespeare excited and rejuvenated. Each return to the text offers further vision into it. Such study *is* self-renewing. For most people, teaching composition does not bring the same feeling of renewal. Composition teaching remains repetitive and routine. It also takes grotesque amounts of time. If you do it for long uninterrupted, it turns your mind to oatmeal. It is no good pretending this isn't so. One of the main problems of composition teaching is just this burnout. How can one design a program that avoids it?—

one that renews the teacher in a cybernetically stable way, as literature does?

Beyond teacher burnout lurk other tarbabies. Get interested in composition and you will find yourself in administration. It comes with the job. The teaching of writing, in the present general campus scene, involves an incredible amount of liaison and planning, far more than a ten-week bout with "English Drama to 1649." And it involves keeping up with technology. As electronic communications technology develops, composition programs will rely heavily upon it. It will stand at the center of what they do. But how do you factor into the regular career-pattern of English studies the computer specialists, TV producers, systems analysts, and statisticians needed for a large-scale, campus-wide composition program?

For these and many other reasons a strong case, both theoretical and practical, can be made for keeping literature teaching distinct from composition. Can an equally strong case be made for bringing the two activities together? Again, first theory and then practice.

Theory. I have argued that the definition of literature which legitimates English studies as an independent discipline—its departmental license— must be discarded if composition is to share more than a Xerox machine with literary study. Strong reasons, even aside from the composition problem, suggest that this required theoretical change might be good for English studies. They suggest, too, a new kind of departmental franchise.

To conceive of literary texts as constituting a separate reality is also to conceive of a positivistic social reality just "out there" and a self just "in here," halfway between the ears. Both concepts have been discarded by almost every other discipline that deals with human behavior, as I argue throughout this book when I talk about the "Post-Darwinian synthesis." Literary critics who still think this way thus find themselves at war with the rest of the curriculum: with the sociologist who examines role-theory; with the cultural anthropologist who finds "ordinary" communication astoundingly full of literary ingredients; with the perception psychologist who stresses the active, participating, integrative role of perception (a role that makes nonsense of the C-B-S theory of prose style, for example); and, above all, with those who study the social behavior of animals and who are finding the sources of literature's mythic energy not in a mystic visionary imagination but in the deeply layered, fundamentally non-intelligent depths of the limbic system. If the composition problem were to force a paradigm change in English studies, one that enabled it to join this new consensus, such a change alone would make the composition crisis worth facing—even, perhaps especially, in English departments that can afford to ignore it.

Practice. The two fields obviously overlap in day-to-day teaching and research—in linguistics, philology, and so on—but we need not linger here when larger issues merit attention. The first of these issues, the undergraduate curriculum, derives directly from our theoretical discussion. The disintegration of the undergraduate curriculum has now been universally remarked. It lacks any legitimating premise except *chacun à son goût.* The current attempts to restore it by reinstating the old breadth requirements and their attendant stale clichés, will all fail. They depend on the same dead paradigm for social behavior that keeps English literature and English composition facing in opposite directions. As I try to show in the next chapter especially, it will be the new Post-Darwinian humanism that will really refound the undergraduate curriculum. Literature departments must choose whether to join this new curriculum to try to assert their centrality within it or whether, like Classics, to paint themselves into their own quiet corner.

The felt center for studying man is shifting from the traditional humanities to other disciplines in much the same way that the traditionally European focus for Western thought has now diffused throughout the globe. In my own field of rhetoric, for example, the exciting discoveries now come from primatology and sociobiology and genetics, not from the academic discipline of rhetoric. This discipline does not even know that it has been usurped. It continues, with a kind of genial, knee-jerk antiquarianism, to—if I may borrow C. S. Lewis's wonderful phrase—"leave no corpse ungalvanized." Meanwhile, life and hope have marshalled elsewhere. If literary studies really should stand at the center of a humanist curriculum—and I think they should—they must be prepared to explain how and why this should be so. A new legitimating premise for the department is required, and also a new day-to-day working sense of what a department is and how it relates to other departments.

For a model we might glance at a discipline like biology which, unlike our own, has fully participated in the Post-Darwinian synthesis. The "department" there is clearly fissionable material, an ad hoc structure that tries to change, subdivide, and readjust to a developing, expanding body of knowledge. At least in the biology departments I know about, the result has been radical and nervous structural reorganization. We need the same thing in English studies. Coming to terms with composition is our best chance to bring it about. The department system, which began at Harvard in 1825 and really caught on at the end of the nineteenth century, has now a long evolutionary history. It works best as it has worked in English studies, when it presides over the *genesis* of a discipline, provides the focus which early growth requires. But in maturity it can strangle the discipline it was created to nurture. Decisions are made for the health of the *department*—a derivative, ancillary unit, remember—and not for the growth of the discipline. When you go this far, you are polishing a dead paradigm. It is arguable, I think, that English studies has now gone this far.

English studies can, then, choose a voice in the new humanism or run back to the old. We face the same choice, on a larger scale, in deciding our role in a multiracial and multilingual America. An English department's sense of itself, its whole manner of proceeding, depends on a society monolingual in English, and idiomatically so. That monolingualism is now changing. Some regions feel the change more than others, but in some degree it will come to everyone. The most obvious revolution comes in the broad band of Hispanic culture that now runs from Southern California across the Southwest, skips first up to Chicago and then down to Florida, and then runs northward to New York and beyond. In California, the Asian-American population provides an obvious second instance; in other places, there are other groups—the West Indian population in Toronto, for example. For the whole country, of course, the native black dialect remains a persistent, if partial, exception to the monolingual premise. Most of these groups are reproducing themselves in greater numbers than the Anglo population and presumably will continue to.

And over these broad, home-grown population changes we must now layer the waves of immigrants reaching our shores. To take as an example my own home ground, Los Angeles now has the largest

Korean community outside Korea, the largest Armenian community in America, a large Iranian community, over a hundred thousand Egyptians, the largest Polynesian community outside Polynesia, well over a hundred thousand Vietnamese, and now a daily influx of Central American political refugees. When earlier waves of immigration hit America, it was a far different America. The melting pot was still supposed to melt; there was no talk on Ellis Island about the right to one's own language. A low-technology agricultural society offered menial and unskilled jobs. There was a lot of vacant land and first-generation industrial growth to act as a cushion. All these absorbent circumstances have now changed, and the language problems have gotten worse—more languages, more different *kinds* of language, and all coming at once.

To such a population, the study of English, and even American, literature is bound to seem alien. For most of them, and for at least a generation, current spoken English will seem difficult enough and earlier stages of the language—the Shakespearean and Chaucerian versions which I customarily teach, for example—impossibly remote. Most of these students, when they reach the university, are not going to major in English. They will study English composition, if we make them, but not English literature. Let me give you another Californian example: 20 percent of the undergraduates at Berkeley and UCLA are now of Asian-American descent; of this group, only 6 percent major in a humanity of any kind. By the end of the 1980s, the 20 percent will have become 50 percent, but the 6 percent majoring in humanities seems unlikely to increase. What does this promise for English enrollments?

But enrollments only introduce us to the real problem. It will be a good while before many of the new ethnic groups come to the university in force. (That under-representation, of course, presents its own grave problems, political and ideological.) The larger question is what role does English studies want to take in a multilingual society. Shall we sit back and assume that the American pressures for monolingualism will solve our problems? Bring us back to the *status quo ante?* Should we try to train the teachers upon whom this monolingualizing burden will largely fall, which would mean a marked departure from our present practice? Or shall we be content, if it comes to that, to shrink into a much smaller discipline, an Anglo Studies Center in a country no longer predominantly Anglo?

The choice depends on the relation with composition. If we choose an active strategy and try to train the imagination of a multilingual society, composition must play a fundamental part in the endeavor. A passive, monastic strategy leads the other way, toward the old self-enclosed paradigm and departmental self-conception. Choosing an active role brings with it many present dangers: uncertainties of training and evaluation, mistakes attendant on new categories of teaching, new applications of what we already know, strange new areas of research. These dangers should not be ignored. They will inevitably blur the focus and disturb the balance of the present departmental and disciplinary structure. But the passive, monastic strategy brings dangers too. Dwindling disciplines usually become sterile, ineffectual, and querulous. As their sense of breadth and purpose shrinks, morale drops and defensiveness increases. A rancid, Luddite, coterie mentality develops. The humanist disciplines abound in this Luddite resentment already. If we decide to hide, it can only get worse.

The relation with composition stands, then, at the center of the basic decisions for English studies: the decision about its place in the humanist curriculum and the decision about its place in a multilingual America. In both cases, these decisions are going to be made. In the past, they have been made for us by a dominant tradition. Not so today. America will have to *decide* on its linguistic reality and *decide* on its definition of man. If English studies wants to take a hand in these decisions, it will have to take an interest in composition. These are not Hobson's choices forced upon us by enrollment pressure. These are broad, considered policy decisions, the decisions humanists are supposed to be especially good at making.

A third decision impends, also, one that comprehends the other two. It is now daily front-page news that the orderly sequence of American education has broken down. The three *R*s usually make the headlines, but the decay of study in other disciplines—history, for example—has been at least as grave. College students read and write like high-school sophomores, law students (if you are lucky) like freshmen, a high-school principal crows with glee when his graduating seniors read at ninth-grade level. The educational sequence in America has, of course, been notoriously disorderly and discontinuous. In a developing America realizing itself westward, such discontinuity literally came with the territory. What is happening now is more than more of the same. The social breakdown of the schools is profound and well-documented, but the intellectual breakdown is even worse. The teaching of literature, our immediate concern, is desperately haphazard and ill-informed. Here a lonely traditional devotee labors to teach Thomas Hardy to an uncomprehending class of world refugees, there a 1960s veteran trooper tries to get a class into *Soul on Ice*.

And the teaching of writing is, if anything, worse than the teaching of literature. How could it be otherwise? Most of these teachers have not been trained to teach either literature *or* composition. Teacher training is, after all, the first thing an ambitious English department discards. The teachers labor with incredible courage and devotion in their impossible new world, without even a training adequate for the old-fashioned possible one.

This pathological lack of orderly sequence demands remedy. We cannot, though, restore the old status quo. Too much has changed. And who, in God's name, would want to restore it anyway? The new curriculum for English must combine language and literature studies in new ways, ways often using electronic intermediation, for a start. If the schools' curriculum is not restored, the college curriculum will continue to be a patchwork of short-term remediation and long-term confusion. Equally clearly, if the schools don't take a directive role in the multilinguistic babble somebody else—business, probably—will step in, the schools will get vouchered out of existence, and the university curriculum will become a total shambles. Both of our larger issues, then—the humanist curriculum and a national language policy—depend finally on restoring an orderly educational sequence in the schools. At the center of this restoration must stand English and Mathematics. Should the well-bred English department take a hand in this restoration? If so, the way in, as in the other two areas, lies through composition. That's where the action has been and is. That's where people are already engaged with the problem. English departments can shape and influence a new English sequence or they can sit back and carp when the job is done—by someone else—so much worse than they could have done it.

Composition, then, embodies the basic choices which English departments must make in the next decade. Not only enrollment pressures stand at issue, but fundamental strategic choices. Circumstances will dictate different choices for different departments. At the center of them all, however, stands a fundamental problem. And this problem, paradoxically, and with a nice, compensatory, egalitarian logic, affects departments more, the *more* research-oriented they are—the *more* remote they are, or think they are, from the literacy crisis. The fear which composition instruction inspires in polite English departments derives partly, as I discussed earlier, from the nonrenewing nature of the teaching. But even more it stems from a threat to accepted patterns of research. Much research in composition has been trivial and jejune, but even had it been better, it has often been of the wrong kind—namely research about pedagogy, about administration, about the delivery systems that socialize knowledge rather than about the research endeavors that synthesize it. It is this threat of *applied* research which, as composition has grown, has sponsored so much fear and suspicion. It is just here, at the pure-applied interface, that the problem needs thinking through.

A university research career, whatever the field, is animated by three kinds of motive: *practical purpose*—how do you kill the tobacco bud-worm but not the crop? *competition*—how can I beat Linus Pauling to the Nobel Prize? and *pure play*—how can I design a simple cubical puzzle that will drive the puzzle-solving world crazy and yet not be actually unsolvable? Different times, different places, and different disciplines have mixed these basic motives in different ways. Practical purpose presides over the Ag School, although rivalry is not unknown there. Competition usually supplies the principal propellant in law schools. The humanities have chosen the play-spirit as tutelary deity, although we often give it a more high-toned name. We are pursuing inquiry, we say, "for its own sake."

The history of education can be schematically but not inaccurately summarized as the effort by educational philosophers to maximize one of these modes and obelize the other two. The Progressive Movement laid all its eggs in the play basket; advocates of professional teaching today, and of the old nineteenth-century moral-gymnasium curricula, centralized the competition motive; the history of "practical" education has taken purposive motivation as referential. Seldom does an educational philosopher urge a radical *mixture* of motives as the ideal situation. Whitehead's *Aims of Education*, for example, pleads this case, but there are few books like it.

The great and exciting periods of research have been those when the three motives worked intensely, and tensely, together. Atomic physics in the decade either side of World War II provides perhaps the best recent example of this tense mixture. The subject displayed the greatest possible theoretical elegance; the competition took place among a small group of geniuses who played off against each other, the personal competition spiced, during the war, by racing Germany for the bomb; and for practical purpose, there was the bomb itself—the extreme instrument for death or the ultimate energy for life. The theory was galvanized and the competition purified by the practical dangers of what Whitehead called the "insistent present." Atomic physics does not provide the only example, of course. We might also cite the history of microbiology research from the early days of the phage group to the discovery of the DNA double helix. There the same rich mixture of motives enlivened the proceedings at every turn. But in all such instances, the structural principle remains constant: in research, both excitement and results come not from the purity of one's motives but from a radical impurity, a dynamic mixture.

If we ask where English studies stands now in this spectrum of motive-mixing, we shall get different answers. If English studies today is suffused by the same excitement that accompanied the Manhattan Project or electrified Watson and Crick's lab at the Cavendish, then literature ought to be left alone and have nothing to do with composition. If, however, English studies stands at the end of an exhausted paradigm, if it is becoming trivialized by hypertrophy of the play motive and acidified by hyperintense competition, then the teaching and study of composition appear in a new light. They offer not a burden but an opportunity. They have to offer exactly what literary studies needs—a big problem, an insistent present. The kind of problem that mixes your motives for you.

Here we pass from questions 1 and 2 on page 110 to a more vexing one—the relation between the two ways to ask the question, the theoretical and the practical. For, if you subscribe to the problem as

I have just presented it, composition practice can redeem and enrich literary theory. The great power of the literacy crisis arises from the enormity of its problem. Research is redeemed by big problems. Big problems are what research is for. The more abstruse the theory, the more it needs a big problem. This is why big second-level university campuses are potentially so much better placed for English studies in the next decade than the reigning aristocrats. *They know the problem in their bones.* They live with it as the context of their literary thinking. *Nocte dieque incubando.* That context changes how literary thinking is done. I believe it is going to change it for the better.

Chapter 8
Post-Darwinian Humanism

All of us who teach about words find ourselves, nowadays, caught up in three overlapping perplexities: a literacy crisis so widespread it has shaken our national self-esteem as an educated democracy; a school and college curriculum that no longer knows what subjects should be studied or when; and a humanism so directionless, unreasoned, and sentimental that it seems almost to quest for Senator Proxmire's Golden Fleece. As I have been maintaining throughout this book, these three areas of endemic confusion are interrelated; they grow from the same fundamental confusion about human motive. Obviously, in proposing to treat these three subjects—composition, curriculum, humanism—I have run a mortal risk. About "humanism," perhaps more decorticated nonsense has been written and spoken than about any other single subject, including God. But close behind comes the curriculum, with composition finishing a strong third. Anyone who proposes to discuss all three, and their relationship, would seem to promise you a sneak preview of what Plato might have called "tedium itself, as in itself it really is." Something fundamental must be happening, to justify reheating these three venerable cold potatoes.

By now it will be clear to readers of this book that I think something fundamental *is* happening—a "Post-Darwinian synthesis." When the returns are in, our whole conception of human motive, and hence of human behavior, will have changed. And that fundamental change will, I think, resolve our present perplexities about composition, curriculum, and the real purpose of the humanities. In this essay I want to recapitulate, and develop further, my argument that a Post-Darwinian perspective can clear up the central misunderstanding common to these three areas of inquiry.

We can begin with composition. The dominant view remains the Clarity-Brevity-Sincerity theory. American rhetoric did not invent this theory, as is sometimes argued—the West's bad conscience about style begins with Aristotle—but we have made the most of it. The C-B-S theory carries three obvious implications for human behavior. First, a nineteenth-century positivist "reality" sits "out there," independent of man's perception, for language to be clear about. Second, since briefer is better, language becomes a means only; the less of it, the better. Third, we all possess a central self—somewhere halfway between the ears, presumably—to be sincere to. In the C-B-S view, language exists to expedite the plain purposes of daily life and must never interfere with them—a view nicely captured by Dionysius' maxim that words should follow thought, not thought words. Such a view splits prose off from verse and nonfictional prose from fictional. It starts exposition and literature pacing off in opposite directions, as if they were fighting a duel.

In the C-B-S view, language remains ideally passive and transparent. Words exert no back pressure on thoughts. The familiar "how do I know what I think till I see what I write," the coaxing of chance all of us depend on, is outlawed. No back pressure from words to self or society is allowed either. We cannot write in order to form the self—it already exists. We cannot write to define a social reality—it already exists too. Self, society, purpose—all exist already. Language simply transmits them from person to person, from monad to monad. The ideal style, in such a view, must be the never-noticed style. But since, in a paradox that seems to have gone unnoticed for two and a half millennia, the style that is *really* not noticed might as well not be there, in fact is not there for the reader who does not notice it, the logical implication of the C-B-S theory is that we should outlaw style altogether.

This C-B-S view of language, usually thought a practical, commonsense one, proves to be just the opposite: extraordinarily impractical. Edenic in fact. You can see this by imagining a day or two lived according to its precepts. Let us imagine that you are a dedicated composition teacher who awakes one day and makes that fortunately rare vow to practice what you preach. The day's first stop is the bathroom, but, alas, your daughter has preceded you there—and is spending a leisurely half hour, to a loud transistor accompaniment, applying her eye shadow. But not for you today the customary compromises of domestic tranquillity. No, today you march under the C-B-S banner of clarity, brevity, and sincerity. And so you bang on the door, open it, tell her clearly and briefly to get out, throw the radio—ah, the sincerity of it—straight through the hall and down the stairs, the Bee Gees first fading with a pleasing Doppler effect and then finishing with a cheerful smash. Once in the bathroom, you take a long and soothing shower, even though it will make you late for work. Not to worry. There will be some C-B-S changes there too. Then cut to the breakfast table, where you notice that your spouse has bought, not the grotesquely expensive English marmalade in which you delight, but the supermarket's plastic substitute at one-third the price. Into the trash it goes, with a clear, brief, and sincere comment about the way of life it so tastelessly symbolizes. And so goes your day. After the first such day, people will be muttering "change of life"; after the second, you'll lose both spouse and job; and after the third, they will come for you with a straitjacket.

The paradoxes of the C-B-S vision of life have not gone completely unnoticed, to be sure. I. A. Richards remarked some years ago in *The Philosophy of Rhetoric* that "neutral exposition is a very special, limited use of language." Ernst Cassirer maintained in the *Essay on Man* that "primarily language does not express thoughts or ideas, but feelings and affections." And Wittgenstein argued in the *Philosophical Investigations* that language exists for social purposes, for "asking, thanking, cursing, greeting, praying." But the message hasn't percolated down to English I. In reaction to this constricted range of expressivity, expository prose has often given way to Creative Writing. Since such writing is done "for its own sake," the C-B-S rules don't apply. In fact, if it is really done "for its own sake," no rules apply at all. How can they, when the writing constitutes its own purpose? This laissez-faire proves handy for the schoolteacher, since beyond "Well, that's nice, Johnny," what can you say about such writing? In such an asocial world, one solipsistic reality is as good as another.

The composition teacher thus faces a conceptual dead end. The C-B-S theory dissolves society, but so does its "creative" opposite. Obviously, since the world hasn't gone completely mad yet, most writing must fall between these two extremes, just where we have no theory to explain it. We have only a C-B-S theory built on a narrow practical purpose and a creative theory built on vague purposelessness.

Turning to the curriculum, we find the same choice of the same extremes. On the one hand, the curriculum should equip students for practical life, teach them a trade or profession. You will recognize here the curricular equivalent of the C-B-S theory. The curriculum should be clear, as short as possible, and genuinely related to the students' real and immediate needs. Against such philistine back-to-basics simplifications, we humanists advance a knowledge-for-its-own-sake argument very like the creative-writing argument—and just as vague. In such a for-its-own-sake curriculum, one pattern or course must be as good as another. And so we have the present situation, a school and college curriculum that resembles nothing so much as a vast department store of the human spirit, an intellectual emporium where the students, each carrying a basket, wander the aisles with the glazed eyes of bewildered shoppers. These two curriculum theories grow from opposed conceptions of human motive, of what human "purpose" means. For the practical training scenario, man is a practical creature who must learn how to build houses, plant crops, and make clothes. For the humanities curriculum, man feels spiritual hungers as well. These hungers, however, remain cloudy and vague in comparison to the nicely demarcated goals of professional training. The practical curriculum has always offered a convincing raison d'être, a carefully ordered sequence of courses, and clear standards of competence. Not since the decay of the classical curriculum has the humanist curriculum known any of these. The curriculum designer, like the composition teacher, must choose between two opposed and mutually exclusive legitimating premises for the curriculum, two kinds of motive, neither adequate to describe ordinary experience.

When we come to the humanities, what they are and what they mean, we must first admit that today "humanities" can mean almost anything. Recently I went to a meeting sponsored by the California Council for the Humanities. The "humanities" were often defined there, as you might expect, and I jotted down the definitions: Conflated, they go something like this:

> Humanists are trained not only to value facts and numbers but to be broad, to generalize; they are principled yet tolerant, firm yet flexible; they not only value individuals and individual facts but have wide interests and put things together; humanists value the constructive play of mind, analyze people but oppose mechanizing them, keep open minds, develop and realize themselves, yet remain

concerned with the eternal quests for love, justice, and the meaning of life; humanists separate the practical and immediate from the spiritual and long-range, means from ends, container from contents(!); relevant but not parasitic, they preserve the humanist tradition and perspective and show a concern for human values, for the value of the humanities, and for the humanities as a national resource; they deplore our current lack of direction in achieving a liberal education and want to see a broader education that will provide the basis not only of a society's sense of rootedness but of its innovation.

The Greeks had a phrase for all this: "hoi autoi peri tōn autōn tois autois ta auta" ("the same people saying the same things to the same people about the same things"). Apart from the tautological platitudes about how humanists humanely humanize humanity, I extracted from this discussion, as from dozens like it I have heard and read, only an unresolved central contradiction: whereas humanists do things for their own sake rather than for profit or direct social purpose, what they do is so vital to society that if they decline for good (and they have been declining for as long as the middle classes have been rising), the commonwealth will go down with them. Humanists insist with equal strength on their own uselessness and on their use, their crucial purpose and their crucial purposelessness; but no one explains how they can have both qualities at once.

The humanities have become a public institution now, with a National Endowment, but the NEH is a bureaucracy without a legitimating theory. No coherent explanation of the humanities' social usefulness has ever been advanced. We get only sentimental pieties like those I have just replayed. The humanists can muster occasional fits of repentance and self-flagellation like those of the 1960s, but they don't seem able to explain their central contradiction, their purposive purposelessness. And the egalitarian social revolution has left them more puzzled than ever, trying to peddle an aristocratic purposelessness to a purposeful mass culture, striving, as it were, to subdivide the Palace of Versailles into workers' flats.

At the heart of our three perplexities, then—composition, curriculum, and the humanities—we find the same basic difficulty: our notion of human motive. On the one side stands straightforward pragmatic purpose—the need for food, shelter, sex, survival—along with the

C-B-S language and practical training that help get the work done. On the other side lurks the misty land of for-its-own-sake behavior. We don't know what such behavior really is or does (the great convenience of the for-its-own-sake motto being that we need no longer ask ourselves this question), but somehow such purposelessness defines the humanities. The arts form part of such behavior but not the whole. Appreciation of the arts—to resurrect a discredited phrase— also forms part, but not the whole. For the rest, we just don't know, and so wander off into tautology and platitude.

I want, just for the moment, to call this undefined area of motive "stylistic" motive. It includes, besides the arts, a wide range of behavior that we often subdivide into categories like "game" and "play." It is stylistic motive that brings our great republic to a halt on Superbowl Sunday, that made us try to save face in Vietnam, that galvanized us collectively to spend billions putting a golf cart on the moon, that leads us individually to spend only slightly less to put a Chippendale chair in our living room or a vintage Porsche in our garage. Of course, since we pride ourselves on being a practical people, we invent practical excuses for these things. Big sports means big profits; we needed to find out whether life existed on the moon, since we might have to live there after we have made the earth uninhabitable; and Chippendale chairs and Porsches are good investments.

We are not alone in fooling ourselves like this, of course. Naive purpose has always been the great utopian delusion in the West. Utopia itself, that ideal state which Thomas More designed and which we continue to revere as a mystical pattern of the pure and purely human life, was constructed to preserve purpose and banish style. I have discussed this at length in chapter 3, above. It is our sharing in this equation of purpose with "Reason" and style with "Pride" that permits us to believe in something as absurd as the C-B-S theory of style, for only in a utopia would the C-B-S composition pedagogy really make sense: the utopian society and the theory share the premise that human behavior is purposive. All the other things that language does in our world, the whole burden of stylistic motivation, would be needless in a utopia because no stylistic motivation would exist there. Creative self-expression would certainly be unnecessary since there would be no self to express. And so with the curriculum.

Only professional training would be needed. Learning for its own sake would not occur, for it forms part of the stylistic motive which utopia abolishes. As for the humanities, they, like the arts at their center, would be banished as completely as they were from the Platonic Republic that More used as a model. Precisely at this point, of course, More stops being consistent. He smuggles arts and letters back in, and then up to the front row. The whole of Utopian purpose labors so that Utopians can spend their leisure in study and reflection, in study, as we say, for its own sake. What More ignores is that, in a wholly purposive society like his Utopia, there would be nothing to reflect about.

This inconsistency has gone unremarked in the commentary because humanists ever since More have cheated in the same way. We have insisted that ideally we are sensible, rational creatures—in other words, purposive—and that if only we would follow that ideal in practice, there would be plenty of time for our humanistic specialty, the non-purposive, stylistic behavior we have just outlawed. We argue for an ideal state—egalitarian, reasonable, wholly purposive—and base upon it a C-B-S writing theory and pedagogy; we then choose an antitraining, antipurpose, for-its-own-sake liberal arts curriculum, which such a state would neither need nor allow. We conceive of humanism as working for a purposive, egalitarian utopia on earth, but one which, once established, would exist only for aristocratic play, to indulge the stylistic motive that it has spent its life trying to abolish. Our composition theory is purposive, utopian; our curriculum theory is anti-utopian, antipurposive, for-its-own-sake; our humanities theory tries to be both at once. No wonder we are perplexed.

To resolve these perplexities, we need to marshal ideas from three different, though overlapping, areas. Though none is absolutely new, all have been transformed in the last hundred years. The first is social dramatism, the second is games and play, and the third has come to be called sociobiology. Let me take them up in that order.

The *theatrum mundi*, all-the-world's-a-stage metaphor has been around for a long time, but beginning with William James's *Principles of Psychology*, it has been entertained with a new literalness. Thus literalized, it implied a new conception of self and of society, a basic reversal of our customary thinking. The self bequeathed to us by the

Judaeo-Christian tradition grows from the inside out. We start, at birth, with a soul, a central essence, which grows and expands as it copes with the world. These central essences, when put into collision (or perhaps I should say "collusion"), create a society. But what if we reverse the flow, and argue—as did George Herbert Mead, for example—that the self grows not from the inside out but from the outside in, that it is created by society. Our felt sense of selfhood, in such a view, comes from enacting a series of roles, building up a self from layers of dramatic reenactment. Instead of possessing a fixed, static self, we must every morning get our act together again. The self, hovering forever in danger of disintegration, is forever knit back together by dramatic reenactment. Such a self will not play a passive role, will not simply encounter experience, but will seek it out, form reality even as it is being formed by it. This conception of a dynamic role-playing self has been elaborated in the last hundred years by many thinkers, from philosophers as various as Dewey, Ortega, Santayana, and Wittgenstein to a stream of social psychologists extending from the original Mead-Cooley generation to modern popular writers like Eric Berne and Erving Goffman. Role playing has become a cocktail party cliché, but without as yet teaching us its central lesson. We have simply assimilated it to the old central self, made "role playing" a trendy name for insincerity.

But a more profound redefinition of human motive has been launched: to the degree that our self comes from society rather than imposes itself on society, we will often act for the sake of acting itself. Acting makes us real, sustains the social drama, keeps us feeling alive. Such behavior is not at all purposive and functional, in the ordinary sense of these words; it is behavior for its own sake. Such a dramatic motive begins to dissolve our central paradox. Behavior for its own sake must always seem mere play, frivolous and useless, so long as our conception of purpose remains purely utilitarian. But if the self is dramatic, then play, behavior for its own sake, changes from ornamental to essential. It creates the purposive self in the first place, provides the raw material for purposive behavior.

This revolutionary redefinition of human motive has been elaborated both conceptually and artistically. By now thinkers in practically every field that considers human behavior have written on games and play. The artistic elaboration started with Lewis Carroll and moved from the satiric paradoxes of Oscar Wilde on through Dada until it found its pure form in Pirandello. Since then, this basic motive reversal has legitimated a broad range of art, from abstract painting and sculpture to postmodernist gestures like Christo's *Running Fence*, Andy Warhol's endless films, and Robert Wilson's even more endless dramas. And as a logical concomitant of the role-playing self has come society as a drama. Again, though, the concept has become a cliché while the basic conceptual reversal it requires has gone unnoticed. As an illustration of how shocking the reversal is, we might consider one of those Robert Wilson plays I just mentioned.

Wilson's seven-act play, *The Life and Times of Joseph Stalin*, demands a cast of 144 amateur players and about twelve hours to perform. I was not present, alas (or perhaps *not* alas), at one of the four Brooklyn Academy productions and so must depend on an account by Calvin Tomkins:

Act I: The Beach
On a bare stage covered with fine sand to a depth of several inches, the Byrdwoman—Sheryl Sutton, wearing a long-sleeved high-neck, ankle-length black Victorian dress, and holding a stuffed raven in her right hand—sits motionless in a chair. A man in red shorts and a red undershirt is seen from time to time running across the rear of the stage against a backdrop of blue sky and clouds. The sound of gulls comes faintly from somewhere in the distance. Gradually other figures appear. Two girls and a boy, nude to the waist and wearing baggy trousers, perform a series of slow movements. A child daubs red paint on the back of the boy, then sits down to play in the sand. . . . A tall man in striped pajamas . . . with a stuffed bird on his left shoulder, hops backward across the stage. A solders' chorus advances from the wings, making a guttural roaring sound and gesticulating (five of the soldiers are deaf children). Queen Victoria comes out and makes the same gestures and sounds, which cause the soldiers to disperse and go off, saying "Okay." A giant fake turtle crawls across, taking twenty minutes to do so. A man enters carrying a live five-foot snake; he hands the snake to a follower, grasps a rope, and is pulled aloft out of sight. There is also a sort of "Greek chorus," whose heads poke up through holes in the stage apron and whose comments on the action reveal rather little, on the whole.

Most of them repeat only the words "Click," "Collect," and "Collecting," while the most prominent chorister, an Iranian girl with thick dark hair and a liquid voice, speaks entirely in Parsi. And throughout this act and the two acts that follow it a straight chair suspended from the ceiling on a wire descends by invisible degrees.

Toward the end of Act I, which lasts a little more than an hour, events reach a climax of sorts. Sigmund Freud and his daughter, Anna, walk on, following the path of the turtle. A figure identified as Heavyman, in a padded white suit, does an extraordinary whirling dance, raising clouds of golden vermiculite dust. Soon after this, the lights dim and, to the music of "The Blue Danube," sixty Southern mammies—in blackface, wearing long red skirts, gray blouses, white aprons, and pillows front and rear—do the famous Wilson mammy dance. . . . When the mammies have waltzed off, the Byrdwoman is left alone onstage. She has been sitting without moving for more than an hour, now and then making a soft sound like a foghorn. The audience, watching her, grows very still. She stands up, so slowly that the movement is virtually imperceptible. She moves forward to a little square table at the front of the stage and—slowly, slowly— places on it a small green statuette that she had been holding, unseen, in her left hand. Slowly, she raises her eyes to the audience, which has maintained total silence. The curtain comes down.*

When a reporter asked Wilson what all this meant, he replied, "Why do reporters always ask such dumb-dumb questions?" (Tomkins, p. 232). The reporter's understandable question and Wilson's quick retort take us to the center of the humanities paradox. The reporter speaks from a purposive conception of motive; Wilson replies from a stylistic conception of motive. For the reporter, society and dramatic imitations of it must make sense, get somewhere, offer some discernible *purpose,* however kinky or obscure. And because there were no obvious meanings in this remarkable performance it must have been precisely the kinky ones that the audience was looking for—unless New York avant-garde audiences have changed a lot recently—when it left the theater at seven the next morning. But Wilson was up to something more radical than kinky obfuscation. He dismissed the whole purposeful expectation. He was not deforming purposive reality by some obscure

* "Time to Think," in *The Scene* (New York, 1976), pp. 232–33.

allegory that only a French structural psychoanalyst could decode; he was not imitating purposive reality at all. Wilson has written a drama that dismisses the three main Aristotelian elements—plot, character, and thought—in favor of the lesser three—diction, spectacle, and song; liberated from plot, character, and thought, the lesser three live for their own sake. In Wilson's world, behavior really does exist for its own sake. The mammy dance is funny and beautiful, and there is nothing more to it. If it seems a social comment—in this day and time how could a chorus line of sixty black mammies, pillows back and front like so many Aunt Jemimas, be anything but a social comment?—then that is our old purposive expectation at work, just the expectation Wilson's choice of such a symbol warns us to discard. The world Wilson creates in *The Life and Times of Joseph Stalin* thus recreates one of humanism's two mutually contradictory premises, the experience-for-its-own-sake argument. Wilson calls humanism's bluff. Yet every humanist I have talked to about Wilson's work reacts with anger at the absence, not simply of acceptably liberal social significance, but of any thought at all. Or they invent, through allegory, an acceptable significance, and so determinedly miss the point.

Wilson's drama is not the only drama, and certainly not the only art, to call humanism's bluff in this way. A world of social behavior for its own sake is just what postmodernist art is trying to create. Andy Warhol's paintings of money and of Campbell's soup cans transform into pure decoration two of the most utilitarian objects conceivable. The huge Mojave Desert earth sculptures of Michael Heizer convert the enormous excavations that usually presage a skyscraper from purpose to play. The seventeen-mile *Running Fence* that Cristo Javacheff built in Marin County does the same thing for the backyard fence. The Centre Pompidou in Paris—The Beaubourg, as it is called—takes all its pipes and conduits, puts them on the outside of the building, and paints them bright colors, thus transforming purposive guts into ornamental splendor. All these works incarnate what humanism has long argued for—life lived for its own sake, purpose metamorphosed into ornament: Not surprisingly, given its fundamental contradiction, humanism has usually replied with, "Well, uh, that's not, uh, quite, uh, what I had in mind."

This new paradigm emergent from social dramatism and depicted by postmodern art promises two different but related kinds of motive—play and game. In the paradigm of purpose, both remain freaks, unpredictable and ornamental. That is why early writers like Johan Huizinga had such trouble describing game and play. Huizinga's pioneering study *Homo Ludens* (which I discussed also in chapter 4) represents, both in its glorious insights and its obvious self-contradictions, the new paradigm struggling to be born. Huizinga saw that two discrete kinds of motive had to be explained, play and game. Play is spontaneous; it comes from nowhere, from the great land of Spontaneity. The many theories that explain it as a rehearsal for "real life" do not, as Huizinga suspected, really explain it at all. At play's center lurks a behavioral wild-card, a kind of motive altogether beyond purposive explanation. But game is easier to understand. Game means competition, and competition forms an obvious part of the purposive world. But is it so obvious? The more Huizinga thought about it, the less purposive it became. The tail seemed to be wagging the dog. Competition seemed stronger than practical purpose, and logically and temporally prior as well. To get purposes fulfilled, houses built, clothes woven, food harvested, culture had repeatedly to tap the competitive urge. Game motive finally seemed to lie outside the purposive paradigm as fully as play. Huizinga vacillated about these two kinds of motive—sometimes he could find purposes, sometimes not—and his predicament, like the reporter's question to Robert Wilson, brings into focus humanism's central paradox. If play and game form a new behavioral paradigm, a conception of motive inexplicable in terms of purpose, mustn't we give up and simply contemplate these activities? When we talk about behavior for its own sake, haven't we arrived at a boundary condition of our conceptual universe?

And if we are not willing just to contemplate game and play, how can we explain where they come from? Well, as a cultural explanation, why not the for-its-own-sake behavior we have just been considering? The concept of social dramatism has been fleshed out in recent years by the study of cultures, often non-Western, that embody this reversal of play and purpose. The most notable of these is Balinese culture, first explored by Gregory Bateson and Margaret Mead and more recently by Clifford Geertz. The Bali that Geertz describes sounds very like the world of Robert Wilson's play.

Geertz writes, in trying to typify Balinese culture:

> "Playful theatricality" perhaps hits near it, if it is understood that the playfulness is not lighthearted but almost grave and the theatricality not spontaneous but almost forced. Balinese social relations are at once a solemn game and a studied drama. . . . Daily interaction is so ritualistic and religious activity so civic that it is difficult to tell where the one leaves off and the other begins. . . . Art, religion, and politesse all exalt the outward, the contrived, the well-wrought appearance of things.*

Geertz goes on to discuss the "radical aestheticism" of Balinese life, pointing out that "all social acts are first and foremost designed to please" and that "morality here is consequently aesthetic at base" (p. 400). Think of it: a culture based on the paradoxes of Oscar Wilde, a total reversal of purpose and play, government and religion existing for the sake of ceremony and not vice versa, the role constituting the essence of self rather than its social dress.

But if we now know more than Wildean aestheticism did about how a "stylistic" culture—to return to my basic term—can actually be organized, how its specific internal dynamics work, the problem of what "game" and "play" really are, where they come from and what they do, still remains. This brings us to the third area in the current revolution of thinking about motive: sociobiology. Only the evolutionary perspective we find there can explain game and play without explaining them away, can suggest what behavior for its own sake really means. I introduce the sociobiological evidence with trepidation. The humanist response to Darwinism remains a mid-Victorian knee-jerk exclamation that "Men are not monkeys!" If you can get over that, a yet deeper cry of pain emerges about the territoriality and aggression hypothesis. I am going to sidestep both these red flags and argue instead that sociobiology's significance for humanism lies in neither of these areas but, rather, precisely in our areas of motive.

* "Person, Time, and Conduct in Bali," in *The Interpretation of Cultures* (New York, 1973), p. 400.

I assume, since it has been *Time*-magazine-cover news, that I need not spell out the sociobiologists' case in great detail.

To put it bluntly, they revived the doctrine of Original Sin, but without the sin. A doctrine with less popular appeal would be hard to imagine: all the constraints of the old Adam but with none of his enjoyable guilt. The Judaeo-Christian tradition objects because man is not born guilty; the modern culturalist tradition of social science objects because man is not born innocent. In the Judaeo-Christian view, things go wrong because man sins; in the culturalist view, they go wrong because man becomes "sick"; but both views preserve a purposive conception of human motive. Their idea of "real" motive remains the one essentialized in Thomas More's *Utopia:* plain purposes without the ornaments of pride. If man does not always behave purely, still this way is his "natural" way, and departures from it are only temporary aberrations. To the sociobiologist, things seem different. The sociobiological argument blends the inherited behavioral dispositions of Christianity with the ethical neutrality of the culturalist view. Homo sapiens brings into the world not Original Sin but an original biogrammar, a set of inherited—that is to say, genetic—predispositions to behave in certain ways. The heaviest piece of genetic baggage, and certainly the most controversial, is a tendency toward hierarchy and status competition, especially among males. This urge, not simply a leftover from our days as paleolithic hunters, represents a much older primate trait. We are also predisposed to pair bonds—to the male-male bonding a hunting primate needed, to male-female bonding, to mother-child bonding, to a range of trading activities that keep the social drama always in action. None of these urges necessarily determines our behavior. Culture improvises on them, varies the basic melodies with infinite inventiveness.

And culture has been improvising for a long time. Homo sapiens's claim to uniqueness lies just here, in the overlapping of our cultural and our biological evolutions. Our uniqueness, that is, lies in the peculiar mixture of cultural purpose and all those propensities left over from a past still genetically present. In the sociobiological view, then, we are unique just because our motives are *not* utopian and unmixed but, rather, radically confounded. All our practical purposes—

food, shelter, clothing, begetting children—are forever being infiltrated and dominated by an obsessive hunger for status. And they are, too, forever being upset by a whole range of other leftover evolutionary propensities, of those impulses to play that I have discussed on pages 43–45 above as "vacuum behavior."

With this familiar phrase, the various stages of our argument begin to cohere. The domain of play that Huizinga sensed in *Homo Ludens* must be vacuum behavior, variously elaborated. Such behavior does not, as Huizinga saw, possess any immediate social purpose or, often, any context either. And so it cannot be purposefully explained. Yet, since the impulse "wants" to fire and will plague us until it does, it forever dislocates plain purpose. And since the behavioral impulse that thus finds expression was certainly necessary for survival in the past, and may still be, it will lend itself to explanation as a rehearsal for purposive behavior. Often it will grow so important as to crowd out purposive behavior altogether and create the Balinese world of ceremonial gesture which Robert Wilson replicates in his plays.

If Huizinga's "play" thus finds in the sociobiological thesis an explanation that preserves its essence and yet really explains it, so his second category of "game" opens up too. If the pressure of our evolutionary past tempts us to convert everything into play, it also tempts us to convert everything into contest, into a status hierarchy. Law becomes from the beginning an elaborate contest that dwarfs simple justice by the ritualized mumbo jumbo needed to obtain it. Business becomes, not the providing of food, clothing, and shelter, but a game that uses these articles as counters. War always wants to metamorphose from purposive struggle into a chivalric display played out for its own sake. Academic research turns into a career game in which (to use Northrop Frye's wonderful simile) publication becomes an automatic means of accumulating merit, like turning a prayer wheel. And so through every aspect of life. Every time we feel an activity being squeezed out of existence, denatured, by the rules that govern it, we are feeling the pressures of status gaming, or of play, or—usually—of both.

If we want to question the sociobiological premise—that Homo sapiens has a biogrammar, genetically programmed behavior patterns—

we can, of course, argue with the experimental data. I myself am not competent to do so. Those who are seem, on the whole, to acknowledge a biogrammar for human beings but to question details of its manifestation. For our purposes, though, a simpler test will suffice. As humanists we are concerned with behavior for its own sake. If man has no genetic biogrammar, where does this behavior come from? A purely culturalist view cannot account for it. Behavior for its own sake presupposes an inherited behavior repertoire, a human biogrammar. No biogrammar, no behavior for its own sake. No behavior for its own sake and, as we have seen, no humanities either.

So sociobiology tells the humanities where their power comes from, what kind of behavior forms their main concern. A purely purposive conception of motive renders the arts genuinely irrelevant to human behavior, and the humanist along with them. But if much human behavior wells up biogrammatically, as game and play, then this nonpurposive range of motive will constitute exactly the humanist's business, whether it manifests itself as "art" or "life." Thus a humanist who stays within the range of play becomes a preacher. In his larger social function, the humanist must relate the two ranges of motive, purposive and nonpurposive, harmonize them, keep them working symbiotically. This orchestration of human motives stands at the heart of politics. Humanism, then, amounts to cultural politics. It does not, like ethics, repudiate the biogrammar; it orchestrates it. It does not outlaw game and play in the name of seriousness but uses them to build a dynamic, perpetually unstable but perpetually renewed, kind of political seriousness.

Humanism's social task begins, then, by making man self-conscious about his motives. It must teach him that he has not simply various motives but two fundamentally different kinds of motive, and it must show him how to distinguish the one from the other. The humanist always keeps one foot in art and one in behavior, cultivating a double concern because man is double. Human nature is forever tempted by its evolving inheritance to play and to compete. Somewhere between these two lies the domain of purpose, a world of practicality that we can, if we are lucky, sustain by balancing the two powerful and opposed urges of the biogrammar. This balancing is the humanist's task. By carrying it out we can *create* purpose and thus find the ultimate usefulness we have so long, and so obscurely, thought ourselves to possess.

Now that we have focused humanism a bit, we can return to its parallel perplexities—composition and curriculum. We saw, in curricular planning, two antithetical designs, practical training and learning for its own sake. The for-its-own-sake impulse we have factored into the two, often contending, urges of spontaneous play and competitive game. The urge to compete has obviously played a central role throughout Western educational history. Our students' obsession with grades looks tame beside the classical emphasis on debate and display. The impulse to play with knowledge, to learn simply because the mind wants to learn, has triumphed less often. Play has always been squeezed between training on one side and winning on the other. It was in response to this double squeeze that the progressive movement in American education emphasized the play impulse in the schools and that the sixties' radicals urged it on the universities. But from the beginning, educational theorists have worked to pare the curriculum down to one legitimating premise. Education should simply be training for life. Or simply mental exercise, the mind, as Santayana put it, playing with its own phosphorescence. Or education should be a miniature competition to prepare us for the big competition, this effort often being expended in extracurricular activities designed to render the curriculum irrelevant.

A pure theory, one built on a single, homogeneous kind of motive, makes educational planning so much easier. We can be consistent, finally see—and say—what education is about. And, of course, we can indulge our own competitive spirit by belittling the other two legitimating premises. But consistency, if our analysis of human motive is accurate, represents exactly what we should avoid. If human motive is radically mixed, composed of what we have come to call purpose, play, and game, and in ever-shifting combinations, then the university curriculum that coordinates these motives ought to preserve a similar dynamic pluralism. We might picture a curricular spectrum with purpose at one end and play at the other and with the spirit of game energizing the whole. Education serves society best when these three kinds of motive are radically mixed by the curriculum. When one begins to dominate, the curriculum starts to decay in a related way. When the competitive urge dominates, the joy goes out of learning. When the play element dominates, a precious cuteness soon prevails, as when progressive education dominates the schools in both practice and theory or when in the university world a particular type of scholarly inquiry becomes stale and inbred. When training (manual or mental) governs, innovation lags and the curriculum ossifies into rigid rules for obsolete jobs. Western education has often exemplified each kind of misguided dominance. Sometimes, indeed, it seems to have done little else. The rare times of greatness have all occurred when the three motives contended with equal vigor.

Thus the curriculum must orchestrate these three motives. The humanist range, narrowly construed, is the play sphere, but by a phrase like "a humanistic background" or "well-rounded liberal education," people really mean a balanced mixture of the three motives, the three legitimating curricular purposes. If you want to define humanism on the curricular level, this mixing must be it. The humanist's job on the curricular level thus turns out—*quelle surprise*—to be the same job that he performs in society at large: harmonizing the different ranges of motive. And by designing a curriculum that does this—curriculum design has not been the great humanist fixation by accident—the humanist will ensure that the school and the university fulfill their fourth legitimating premise, the education for citizenship. For what is civility but knowing how to balance one's own ranges of motive, knowing that these different kinds of motive operate in other people as well? Making play, game, and purpose work together is what government, at any level, comes down to. Again, humanism *is* politics.

And so humanist teachers ought to resist not only the business world's demand that education be made all practical purpose but also their own predilection for making it all play. The two sides must contend, and in the competitive spirit of game. Western education has not approximated this ideal often, but American education has done as well as any. Our characteristic impulse has always reached toward mixed motives, big all-purpose high schools and multiuniversities. But recently the legitimating motives have been allowed to separate and go their own ways. They all remain on campus, but we can't agree on a formula for mixing them. We fail partly because we lack a clear vision of what the fundamental motives are and partly because no one formula can guarantee the mixing. This is just where Robert Maynard Hutchins went wrong, as did many others. No one pattern of subjects will guarantee the essential kind of mixing. You can study great books for nongreat reasons. If we agree on a core curriculum again for the first two undergraduate years, it can be taught in a preprofessional way that destroys the mixed-motive intent. A genuinely humanistic curriculum provides not only a set of subjects but a spirit of inquiry, and this spirit comes embodied in individuals, handed down one-on-one, as an intuitive attitude toward learning. Maybe this intuitive attitude is what we mean by "talent for teaching," a sense of how play, game, and training can be mixed in a—can I use the word?—"humanistic" way. And maybe this is why teachers with such an intuitive balance can "humanize" almost any curriculum, save us from our most successfully outré designs, give students the balanced—again can I use the word?—"humane" view of life they hunger for.

It begins to be clear, I hope, how the triply mixed conception of motive that informs Post-Darwinian humanism illuminates the composition course as well. When I called the nonpurposeful range of motive "stylistic," it was with the composition course in mind. For the decision about style in prose corresponds exactly to the decision about motive we have just been rehearsing. The C-B-S pedagogy is based, as we have seen, on purposive motive. At the opposite end of the motive spectrum stands the prose that plays with words for their own sake, whether in third-grade word games or Nabokov's *Ada*. The legitimating premise for this self-consciously playful prose stands the C-B-S theory on its head, assumes a world where words determine thought. And over the whole spectrum plays the spirit of game, of "scoring," as Robert Frost called it. The writing course, when it actually works, mixes all three motives just as the curricular purposes mix in good teaching. The study of prose thus provides, once we understand it aright, a model for motive. It can, then, act as a do-it-yourself curriculum guide, can do something for students besides sharpen their verbal pencils.

To give students a comprehensible and comprehensive theory of style means giving them at the same time a theory of motive. I have been arguing here for Post-Darwinian motive, a theory that sees human affairs as legitimately propelled by game and play as well as by purpose. This implies, for the writing course, a training in writing, imitating, and parodying all kinds of prose, not just transparent essays that model the C-B-S philosophy. Only when the students write in a range of prose styles that models the range of their felt motive will they begin to think that English I might also be useful after school. The creative writing alternative reveals just this urge toward stylistic motive, an urge touching all human experience, not just the purposive part. The Post-Darwinian perspective illuminates the hungers that creative writing feeds. And once we acknowledge the full range of human motive, the split between exposition and creative writing heals itself.

The decision about style, then, means a decision about motive. If this is so, teaching students to write means making them self-conscious about their own complex motives, their layered purposiveness; and it opens the way, finally, to a genuinely integrated curriculum. For the same decision about motive—the same attempt to keep separate practical purpose, the competitive impulse of game, and the vacuum behavior of play—characterizes every discipline that deals with human behavior, from aesthetics to population genetics.

At the center of Post-Darwinian humanism stands the model for motive we have been discussing. If we can teach it effectively in the composition course, we'll be giving our students a conceptual framework that will allow them to find, and to create, some order among the humanistic disciplines. They will be able to recognize, when they read about Bali in anthropology, a kind of motive they already know. When they argue about how prose style works in historical writing, they will point out to their history professor that, since behavior itself is often stylized, style in a historical narrative constitutes itself a kind of reality. They will have met role theory before they get to it in sociology and will have a conceptual framework for it. When they learn about Dada in their art history course, they will remember Bali—and Nabokov. And they will know that they are learning about morality in art history as well as in ethics. They will also be much too clever to buy any simplistic utopia like More's, based on a naive sense of human purpose.

The composition course, in such a view, becomes not a course in peripheral skill but one in central concepts. It becomes, in fact, the centerpiece in the humanities curriculum. I know that, struggling as we all are with literacy on a much lower plane of regard, such centrality may seem a fond dream. It is not. It provides just the legitimating premise which the teaching of writing has lacked.

And, unlike the C-B-S pencil sharpener, it provides a banner you want to fight under. For what I have chosen to call Post-Darwinian humanism explains an act of harmony we have been trying to perform all along but have not really understood. The Post-Darwinian paradigm is not so utterly new after all. Post-Darwinian humanism advances the argument for verbal training that the rhetorical paideia has stood for since classical Greece. Rhetoric has always argued that verbal training provides the central model for motive. It has always insisted that competition is the father of all things, verbal play the mother— and everyday purpose the child of these mighty opposites. The Post-Darwinian synthesis has now provided an empirical explanation for this mythical account, for what the rhetorical paideia has been trying to do all along. It allows all of us closet sophists to understand our own subject for the first time.

At the beginning of the *Gorgias,* Plato has Socrates ask Gorgias about the theoretical basis of his art, what *technē* rhetoric possesses. In the wonderful world of Platonic dialogue, rhetoric never answers back to Socrates with anything except strawman silliness. But we can answer back now. Post-Darwinian humanism gives us the behavioral basis for rhetorical study, makes clear, at long last, where the *technē* of rhetoric comes from. For the first time we can see what the rhetorical paideia is all about and how it can be used, as we have always wanted to use it, to organize and legitimate the humanistic curriculum. The details will take a while to work out, but this enterprise makes the study of rhetoric challenging as it has not been since the Renaissance. Not only the pedagogy of writing but the whole humanities curriculum must be done over, and the study of rhetoric will stand at the center of it. I don't for a moment underestimate our desperate present crisis in literacy and the humanities. But amidst its pressures we can at last begin to glimpse what English teaching is for, the "sake" in "for its own sake." And we can see that it is not only, and finally, a pedestrian and safe effort to teach basic skills but an extravagantly romantic attempt to give the full Western self to everyone. Our enterprise has now, whatever the difficulties, both a clear conceptual framework and a noble goal; we can see, if not a grail, then at least a challenge cup and the road toward it. And that is why I, for one, am full of excitement—and of hope.

Chapter 9
Composition, Literature, and the Core Curriculum: The UCLA Writing Programs

The Core

Instruction in writing, if it is to be more than simply an ancillary service to other kinds of instruction, finds its natural home in the first two years of the undergraduate curriculum. These two years have been a notorious shambles for a decade now, and they have never really had an informing purpose or natural shape since the characteristically American university took form a hundred years ago. The upper division possessed the essential departmental and disciplinary core to evolve along coherent lines. Not so these first two years. Nobody knew what to do with them. Give them back to the secondary schools? Veblen recommended this in one way, and Hutchins in another. (Veblen wanted to give the introductory instruction back to the schools; Hutchins to bring the schoolchildren to the subjects.) Make them a long preparation for the major? Engineering and some of the life sciences tried this path. Drop one and make the other preparation? Nicholas Murray Butler thought that might work at Columbia.

The central trend of thinking, though, went in a more positive direction. To decide what is the non-negotiable center of a liberal education, and make that general education the focus of the first two years, a necessary and balancing propaedeutic to the specialization of the last two. This could be done in a specially designed program that laid down an unvarying pattern which each student had to follow. Alexander Meiklejohn's experiment at Wisconsin aimed at this solution to the problem, and so did the college curriculum at Chicago, the Directed Studies Program at Yale in the early 1950s, Tussman College at Berkeley in the 1960s, and a number of other attempts. In the strong form, this solution specified a series of Great Books, as at Saint John's, where the curriculum took over all four years. In the weaker form, only a series of general education courses was specified, the Great Books read within them being left to local

144

option. Harvard and Columbia are cases in point here. In the weakest form, the non-negotiable core became the familiar series of breadth requirements; here students had only to take some course of some kind in some basic subject areas. Sometimes this pattern was defined to make sense. Usually so many courses could satisfy the requirement (over six hundred at UCLA in 1981) that the requirement simply evaporated.

All these efforts to define a "core" for the first two years shared a simple unstated and unexamined premise. They were trying to build the core from the outside, to establish a center by building an external structure. They all wanted to lay down the campus sidewalks where Symmetry and Wisdom said they should be and then make the students walk on them. Symmetry and Wisdom, however, could never agree on where the sidewalks should go. Everyone could agree on nutritious, enfranchising platitudes about the "whole person" but not on what curriculum was to spank this baby into life. The endless (truly—they still continue) faculty debates revealed only that there was no core of commonly-agreed-on liberal learning. The programs that tried to legislate such a core all ran into trouble. And all on the same trajectory: after a year or two, the faculty got bored with teaching general courses and wanted to go back to their own disciplines and career games. The faculty wanted to wear its own paths and then pave them. So did the students, who looked on the required courses as a tiresome chore. The General Education Program at Harvard, begun by the famous "Red Book" report of 1945, ran into both faculty and student ennui that finally brought it down. The Yale Directed Studies Program hung on but dwindled into eclipse. Berkeley's Tussman College folded. And so on. And now, at the beginning of the 1980s, we are starting *exactly the same cycle again*. This resurrection provides a classic case of what Kuhn calls a dead paradigm. Everything has been said and none of it begins to solve the problem.

The rhetorical, sophistic, Darwinian definition of style which the earlier essays in this book develop suggests both why the paradigm has died and what an alternative one might look like. The thinking about the core has been all "serious" rather than "rhetorical" thinking, all *Through* and very little *At*. No combination of *Through* texts, no patterns of "serious" thinking, can capture the essence of Western culture because that essence lies in just the multistable oscillation between the two kinds of thinking and writing, views of individuals and society, which the basic assumptions of the "core" thinking have proscribed at the beginning. Every "core" I have ever heard of begins with Plato—and never goes any further than him. The Sophists are dismissed in just the way Plato had hoped, and the rhetorical perspective and range of motive never return. Thus no effort of this sort can succeed, can agree on a core. And yet the core, the essence, is right there staring us in the face. This essential oscillation of *At* and *Through* vision, which in our first renaissance Castiglione called *sprezzatura*, can be taught through any of the great literary or philosophical texts of Western culture. The oscillation is what makes them great. To make sense of them, all you need is a theoretical matrix like that developed in chapter 5. Then, with texts put together in all kinds of combinations, you avoid the boredom that so soon descends on general education and classical civilization courses.

The historical beginning of such a course obviously would be the quarrel between Plato and the Rhetoricians, presented fairly for the first time, with Plato's grotesque misrepresentations back-lighted by analysis and commentary. But we don't need to begin here. The essence of this quarrel is renewed at regular intervals in Western intellectual history. It is, in fact, what that history is all about. We can begin by juxtaposing More and Castiglione, as I have done in chapter 3, or by contrasting Dante and Chaucer, or George Eliot and Oscar Wilde. The "core" of the core must be the oscillation that established the complex Western self. This must be taught, but it can be taught in innumerable ways. The more ways the better. It can be taught in the most minute details of stylistic analysis as well as in the broadest comparisons of theme and structure. One thus avoids with a single step all the protracted and sterile debates about which texts are canonical and which not, which periods and subjects essential and which derivative.

We also avoid the whole problem of trying to design a core structure from the outside; we design from within. We give the student a compass and sense of direction, not a paved path. We give him or her the means of relating "humanistic" disciplines that I suggested in chapter 8. And with such a principle of internal guidance, "core" problems vanish. The new paradigm uses the emerging outlines of our evolutionary nature to reach back to the beginnings of Western culture and show how we have been grappling with that nature in ways as various as the Greek rhetorician's *polemos patēr pantōn* ("struggle is the father of all things"), Christian theology's Original Sin, and the Romantic theory of the isolated, heroic self. And it traces this strand of thinking right through every branch of contemporary social science, and from there into the anatomy and chemistry of the brain. The much deplored split between the sciences and the humanities, C. P. Snow's two cultures, proves to have been a convention of academic life and not a distinction inherent in the nature of things.

As I have said, the more ways of teaching the "core"—the essential oscillation—the better. My own way of doing it is easy to guess: start with the Rhetoricians and Plato, then talk about the oscillation of the self as reflected in the speech-narrative-speech-narrative alternation in Thucydides, then start reading forward in the great literary texts until you come to Post-Modernism in art, our current return to a rhetorical view of life, at the same time reading from the present back to Vico in the texts of social science.* I am familiar with the objections to Konrad Lorenz's arguments about territoriality, but try reading the case for it while you are reading Homer and see if sparks don't fly. Or try, as I have done, assigning Niko Tinbergen's description of the herring gull's courting rituals while at the same time reading the Elizabethan sonneteers. If you are not careful, your students may begin to think that they live in a world not divided into separate courses. My way depends on my interests. It may not be yours. No matter. We have the whole Western tradition before us and all of modern inquiry. But now, rather than Milton's "asinine feast of sow thistles and brambles," it seems a map we know how to read, a voyage we can take without getting lost.

Such a "rhetorical" core—built from the inside out, dynamic instead of static in its essence, avoiding the tedium of canonical texts—sidesteps the old pattern of inevitable failure. But how to get such a core started? The behavioral theory on which it is based is only now

* I have tried to point some lessons of this sort in *The Motives of Eloquence* (New Haven, 1976).

being formulated. We have a dozen years of academic discussion ahead of us before the "humanist" folk in charge of thinking about core curricula will come to see that, for our new renaissance, Castiglione's utopia holds infinitely better promise than More's. What should we do in the meantime? Wait patiently while we rehearse another cycle of dead-paradigm debate about the curriculum? Live through another dozen years with the undergraduate curriculum in pieces?

The earlier essays in this volume have suggested, I hope, a way of thinking about verbal style that makes it a central rather than a peripheral part of undergraduate education. This study of style is the study of a whole range of human behavior, and an essential one if we are to feel ourselves whole. To think about style in this evolutionary way is to envisage it as itself a core curriculum in miniature, providing on a smaller scale the oscillation between serious and rhetorical worlds that we are talking about. To think in this way suggests that, in embryo at least, a dynamic core curriculum *already exists* on campus— in the composition course. Furthermore, to think of style in the evolutionary way implies that the gap between composition and literary instruction, so hallowed in practice, is not an essential theoretical one but a matter of pedagogical custom, academic prestige rankings, and pure happenstance. There exists a common body of thinking, in other words, which could bring composition, literature, and the humanist curriculum into relationship.

Composition provides both the most expedient and the most logical place to begin the reconstruction of the undergraduate curriculum. At the center of a composition course should stand just the oscillation between two kinds of vision, two kinds of behavior, which the core curriculum will continue on a larger scale. Surely the reason we think a training in prose style is so important is that, in its rhythms of writing and revising, it models the oscillation from central to social self, from *Through* to *At* vision and back, which constitutes the full Western self. Here exactly lies its "humanizing" function. Again, an infinity of curricula can perform this function. Good teachers build their patterns into their teaching whatever the curriculum. Isn't this what we mean by good teaching?

The writing course thus forms the perfect introduction to whatever course or courses we assign the function of making the "core" clear, giving the undergraduate students their curricular compass. The two courses are part of the same sequence—a real sequence proceeding from a shared view of life, not an arbitrary compromise agreed upon by a committee too tired and bemused to argue any further. And whatever writing is assigned in the second two years ought somehow to participate in the same view.

So, I think, would run a sketch of what the Post-Darwinian humanist curriculum might look like, of how it might offer a new paradigm. It argues for the teaching of writing as rightfully propaedeutic to a humanist curriculum as well as central to it. It corrects the long Platonic distortion. It heals the embarrassing split between composition classes legitimated by a pure *Through* theory and literature classes legitimated by the opposite *At* kind of priority. It tells the students how they themselves can make sense of the supermarket of courses they will be passing through. Above all, it allows, indeed encourages, the fullest scope to both the teacher's way of teaching and the student's way of learning.

Books First, Action Later

This kind of curriculum is an action-program. It has to be put into practice to exist. Unlike the Platonic design, it does not invite disinterested contemplation. *Sprezzatura* makes sense only as a happening, not as a concept. This is why the Sophists walked the streets instead of the groves of Plato's Academy, and why they taught politics—for this is what they taught—and for money. And this is why they promised results in the here and now and not in a world of immutable ideas. But how do you create a similar action-program today?

I am a university professor and so the answer was clear. Books first, action later. This was, oddly enough, probably the right way to proceed. The basic reversal of thinking required for such a curriculum was so unfamiliar, so fundamental, and so disturbing that the arguments needed to be spelled out in detail before the evolutionary framework made any sense. And even then there was sure to be lively resistance from one's colleagues. The C-B-S theory of prose style has enormous appeal. It is plain, blunt, easy to understand, bottom-line—and partly true. To suggest that it was only partly true, however, was to imply truths about human behavior that most people preferred not to know. As one essayist on the philosophy of Post-Darwinist thinking has put it, "man's behavior was the last of his characteristics that he wanted placed into an evolutionary context."* This was not only because of the satiric reduction which followed upon seeing how little we really are creatures of purpose; there was a genuine evolutionary explanation—at least in the domain of style—for the reluctance to abandon the Platonic simplification. We depend on stylistic communication of all sorts—most notably, of course, nonverbal communication—to supply us an unfakeable code. Life does not permit us always to present our bona fides or to explain fully our attitudinal penumbra. We have to imply them, and we can depend on the reliability of that implication, both as sender and receiver, because it is subconscious, intended but not deliberately so. If we think about this code, it becomes conscious and hence fakeable and hence undependable. It is far more adaptive, if I may use the word loosely, to leave it in the unconscious areas of immediate response. Conscious processing means delay and there just is no time for it.

To these sources of opposition—and they have proved to be as contemptuous and uncomprehending as they are fierce—we must add another, fortuitous rather than essential, but nonetheless strong for all that: the specialized languages of professions. Departments and disciplines vary greatly in their warmth toward the "Great Reversal" that evolutionary thinking implies about human behavior, but they stand as one about the implications for verbal style. Disciplines that deal with human behavior want above all to be thought scientific, and this means a C-B-S theory of prose style. The style used in any one discipline is perfectly neutral and transparent, aims only to give the facts in an unbiased order. That, at least, is what its professors want to believe. The styles actually used, of course, aim first at professional responsibility and disciplinary coloration. They don't want to be clear so much as decorous, pious—just like the rest of us. But

* Richard D. Alexander, "The Search for an Evolutionary Philosophy of Man," *Proceedings of the Royal Society of Victoria* 84 (1971): 95–119.

here this cannot be admitted. For other disciplines, well, . . . of course. What else would you expect? But for our group—the living truth, transmitted in neutral verbal capsules. Even the translation of this kind of professional language into really neutral prose—or as close as we can come to it—is read as satiric reduction. Translate Talcott Parsons into English and, the prose pathologists agree, there's not much left. But nobody wants to hear this. It is too threatening.

Professional language has developed for explicable and legitimate reasons, but professors don't want to admit that these reasons have to do with competition, convention, or anything that might be called a genetics of style. So when I thought of beginning a composition program it was in a climate that suggested caution: one should write books, conduct modest experiments in one's classes, and wait until the times do alter. And there was yet another reason to proceed cautiously. As composition studies become more respectable in the university, they become more research-oriented—and vice versa, since research is what the university respects. The great advantage of composition studies should be their hands-on practicality, but that advantage is being thrown away, just as education schools threw it away two or three decades ago.

It was in February 1979, in the middle of a meeting full of deans, vice-chancellors, and spear carriers like me—I was chairman of the Composition Committee in the English Department—that I found myself offering to start a campus composition program. William Schaefer had returned from running the MLA hyperaware of the literacy crisis; the faculty, in a series of planning conferences, had shown itself equally sensitive to the problem. Now a series of "task forces" was being proposed to study the problem. The flapdoodle this would generate seemed likely to go on forever, and so I proposed a few simple things we could do while the study groups were admiring the problem, and told the astounded multitude how much these would cost. Schaefer is my friend, but he is also a statesman who knows when he has hooked his fish, and so he didn't say anything at all during my outburst against the task forces. He just wrote down my numbers. When I had finished, he said, as the executive vice-chancellor can, "Dick, it looks like I owe you $167,000." I said, "Why not round it off to $175,000?" and he did, and we were off. If I wanted

to try straightening out the undergraduate curriculum and putting
literature and composition into logical relationship with it and with
each other, I had the right place to start.

Now what was I going to do?

Well, several things were clear. First and foremost, I would design
no utopias, mine or anybody else's. The separate-college/separate-
program/little-academy format just did not work. The programs were
hellishly hard to teach, wonderful to take (I knew—I had been through
one), and never lasted. Besides, they were exactly what the non-
Platonic world I was coming from did not recommend. And to try
to impose one on a campus as big (34,000 students) and as heterogeneous as UCLA was not only impossibly arrogant but incredibly
foolish. There would, then, be scarcely any theory at all to begin
with. If the kind of "core" I had in mind was really valid, it would
grow from events. Composition instruction, for the reasons I have
described, would provide a fertile ground, but initially that was all
it could do. Meanwhile, there were a lot of obvious things that needed
doing. As for theory, the C-B-S orientation, with all its warts, would
do just fine, at least for a while. The larger orientation, the global
diagnosis of the problem, would prove useful in the long run. It
might work in the short run too, perhaps, as a reassurance that we
knew what we were doing and where—if the airplane flew—we
were trying to go. But the program would be the opposite of ideological
or doctrinaire. A rhetorical orientation, unlike a Platonic one, cannot
be imposed from above. It has to grow from the needs of ordinary
daily behavior. The UCLA Writing Programs would have to succeed
in terms of immediate institutional needs and the curricular theory
develop from them. "Action First, Books Later," it would be, then,
and not vice versa.

The UCLA Writing Programs

I have been considering up to now the theoretical issues that lie
behind the place of composition teaching on today's university campus.
That theoretical thinking led me to seeing a composition program as
central to the reconstitution of the curriculum. But now I had to
create a program that would work. I could not forget the theory—

it should, at one remove or another, inform all we did—but I could not always think in terms of it either. I had to respond to present circumstances if the whole enterprise was even to get off the ground. I would return to the curriculum theory later—as I will do in this chapter. Now, though, I was in for two years of detailed planning. This planning is as much a part of the story as the theory; core curricula of the sort I am trying to set forth always start from present circumstance and grubby detail. What follows, therefore, is a detailed description of a process in which details were essential. If you find parts of it too detailed, skip them. Utopias, because they describe what ought to be, can choose their details for human interest and philosophic significance. In starting the Writing Programs we did not—more's the pity—have this choice.

My charge was clear and simple: to design a composition program that would "make a noticeable difference to the writing done by all the members of the UCLA community." This community was a citylike cure of sixty thousand souls. It included, besides student writing, a lot of administrative and staff penmanship as well. (There were, I was to learn, over seventy-five professional editors working on campus to handle this output.) First, we needed to survey the problem. Did UCLA in fact have a "literacy crisis"? Did it think it did? During 1979–80, a staff research associate visited every department and every graduate and professional school on campus. I was told on all sides that we should conduct a scientific, statistically valid survey. This was the last thing I wanted to do. It would take forever and it wouldn't really prove anything. Instead, I sent the most tactful, engaging person I knew to talk to people about their writing problems and to collect examples of the writing done on campus.

The results began to emerge almost immediately, although the survey lasted all year. Some findings were as expected. The students had done very little writing in high school. The problem began there and, in the long run, would have to be solved there. But we also found, to our surprise, that students did amazingly little writing at UCLA. And that small amount was shrinking fast to a diet of hour tests and exams. Even here the essay exam was feeling pressure from the factual inquisition. We found everywhere we went that people felt they had a new, and bad, problem with student writing. The examples of student writing we collected confirmed our own English department experience. Again to our surprise, though, we found that the writing problem was felt even more strongly in the graduate and professional schools than at the undergraduate level. This rang a loud warning bell. Graduate student teaching assistants do 40 percent of the undergraduate teaching at UCLA. If they had writing problems— and they did—then the problem extended all the way up to the faculty. We needed to teach the teachers too.

We also became aware, as we had not been before, of the enormous amount of administrative and staff writing that goes on at a large university. We learned about this informally but in convincing if not statistically significant ways. When we began a course in practical writing for business and government, the director of the hospital computer center called up. Could he take it, together with his staff of six? I had not even known that there was a hospital computer center, much less that it had a seven-person writing problem. Meditating on the administrative writing problem raised our consciousness about an associated one: businesses that hired UCLA graduates needed people who could write. I had thought of a university as offering specialized training in writing only for creative writers. This way of thinking, clearly, did not begin to diagnose the problem.

While the survey was teaching us these lessons, I had to start up an office. I had never done anything like this before, but running a program out of my satchel seemed to hold no long-term promise, so I borrowed a room and hired a secretary. We were in business. In December 1979 I put into a memo my thoughts about what kind of business it was. It had, it seemed to me, three basic premises:

1. *The writing problem has been caused by a failure in educational sequence.*
This means that we face two distinct but related problems: (a) a short-range problem—to remedy deficiencies which in a properly-sequenced curriculum would not have arisen; (b) a long-range problem—to restore proper sequence to the English curriculum, and to the writing parts of other courses.

The short-range problem (a) creates some unusual difficulties. It is often objected that these basic skills are "not the university's business." These objections are generally valid but presently irrelevant.

Basic skills are the university's business right now because our students don't possess them and we cannot, for pedagogic as well as political reasons, either dismiss the students or ignore their failures.

But these objections, however unconvincing now, do point to several future difficulties.

First, *staffing*. The remedial reading and writing problem, although real right now, cannot be allowed to become a permanent university task without undermining the whole sense of orderly sequence in the American educational system. If, then, the problem must be defined as temporary, we cannot hire permanent staff to cope with it. We must estimate how long the remedial need will last and devise staffing methods, outside the normal tenure/security of employment system, which will allow us to phase out the program when the need has disappeared.

Second, *the need to restore sequence*. The only convincing answer to the "it isn't the university's business" objection is a plan to restore a reasoned sequence to writing instruction from kindergarten through college, and thus to ensure that in the future elementary instruction will indeed not be the university's business.

Third, *the old sequence cannot simply be reestablished*. New circumstances—minority culture demands, new types of professional language, the TV culture, and so on—will demand a new kind of sequence, one with a new curricular theory and new textbooks. Devising this new sequence *is* the university's business. So is preparing teachers for it. Regular staffing is thus possible here.

We can measure the cleverness of our planning by how well we use the short-term emergency to clarify and hasten restoration of the long-term sequence. Can people hired for the short-term purpose be moved over to the long-term one? Can what we learn from emergency teaching be used to plan writing sequences which will ensure that the next generation is not similarly illiterate?

2. *The writing problem, because of this failure of sequence, is not simply a remedial problem for beginning freshmen.*

Community college transfers are having increasing difficulty meeting UCLA writing standards, and so are our own regular upper division students. Graduate and professional student-teachers don't know how to teach writing or, in many cases, how to write themselves. The high-school sophomore writing at 2d-grade level now finds a counterpart in the young lawyer writing like a high-school sophomore.

3. *The writing problem is a campus problem, not simply an English department problem.*

The traditional response to bad writing is to blame the English department for not doing its job. But no one Freshman English course can cure a problem of this magnitude. Students must learn to write before they come to UCLA and continue to write throughout their years here. All cannot be put right by a one-shot "Freshman Comp" inoculation. Nor is it reasonable to expect the English department to devise and staff the new kinds of courses required. For the most part, instruction of this sort has not been part of the career-pattern of major university English departments. They have traditionally concentrated, as they do now, on literary history and criticism and have resisted becoming a "service department" whose main business is to purvey writing instruction to other disciplines. Composition is not an intellectually respectable area of concentration in English studies, and a concern with textbooks and curriculum does not provide an acceptable alternative to traditional literary research. Major English departments—and this includes UCLA—have very few professors on their staff either interested in or prepared to work in the area of composition. As a result, staffing a writing program through regular appointments in the English department is not possible. Such appointments would distort the department's shape and purpose as a nationally known research faculty. People working in composition would not meet the expected research requirements and could not expect normal advancement. A new kind of organization is needed, an avowed "service department" to perform this needed campus service.

The services we needed to perform, at least at the beginning, were of two sorts. We needed to coordinate the writing instruction currently going forward on campus and we needed to begin new programs. The coordination was long overdue, but I had to tread lightly. Programs that had sprung up ad hoc and thriven were naturally wary of being absorbed into a larger organization. And there were a number of these programs: a Learning Skills Center, a Freshman Summer Program, a very large tutoring program, writing courses given in Extension, a California Writing Project on the Bay Area model, an annual writing conference for teachers, and so on. All these activities had grown to meet specific needs and, except where those needs overlapped, they rarely got together. They certainly formed part of no larger campus strategy and, as I found, the people staffing them often felt voiceless and isolated. These programs themselves were funded and supervised from several different campus fiefdoms, and this did not make co-ordination any easier.

New programs were needed, too, as well as attempts to pattern and streamline what we already had. Most obviously we needed to improve our relations with the secondary schools. *Begin* relations would be more like it, for in the area of composition we had no real working contact with the schools at all. A few people at UCLA knew a few people in the schools, largely through the pioneering work of the California Writing Project, but there was no methodical and continuing liaison between the two. It was bizarre. The undergraduate vice-chancellor had made a beginning, by working with the directors of the local California Writing Project and by holding the annual Chancellor's Conference on Composition. That, however, was one day a year. The problem of improving the teaching of writing in the public schools is enormous. For us, though, just the problem of getting to know what the problem was and who was trying to solve it seemed enormous. The Los Angeles Unified School District has over half a million students and that was only one of the districts sending students to UCLA. In English studies, at least, UCLA had neglected its feeder schools for so long that any sudden attention was viewed with suspicion. All that the schools heard from the university was carping criticism, professors suggesting facile solutions for problems they didn't begin to understand. To come from the university world was to be, in the beginning at least, from the enemy camp. The Rockefeller Commission on the Humanities, in its recent report (*The Humanities in American Life*), has urged "that colleges and universities encourage their faculty to help improve education in the humanities in high schools." Hard to do. The gulf between the university world and the world of the schools is just that—a gulf.

So it was with no illusions about rapid progress that a staff member was engaged to start a schools program for us. She visited dozens of schools, talked to the L.A. Unified's annual meeting of English department chairpersons, began a series of in-service workshops and seminars, a two-week summer seminar, and generally found her way around. She had for many years been a teacher herself and knew the magnitude of the task before her. But we all knew that if we did not reconstitute a link between school and college, we would be in the remediation business forever.

We were certainly going to be in remediation for a good while in any case. We thus began planning an experimental remedial sequence in English (and Mathematics) to see if we could carry forward throughout the freshman year the special instruction we were already giving in the Freshman Summer Program. The new sequence, called the Freshman Preparatory Program (wittily subtitled FP^2, since the committee which created it met in the Mathematics Building), offered in its English composition segment a new curriculum and set of readings which aimed to teach the students the kinds of discourse they would have to produce at the university. With this it coupled intensive counseling and tutorial work and careful curriculum planning. Even the best student was likely to get lost in the maze of the UCLA curriculum; the disadvantaged students were sure to. We would try to teach them the rules of the game, from the basic skills to the styles of academic discourse, from the catalog requirements to the mores and accommodation techniques of undergraduate life. We spent 1979–80 designing FP^2; its director wrote the syllabus that summer; and we began it with two hundred students in the autumn of 1980. In that first year we began, as well, a number of other programs aimed at particular campus needs:

- Experimental sections of the basic freshman course
- A year-long sequence in practical writing and editing
- TA training seminars for TAs in departments other than English
- Special writing courses for high-level administrators
- Seminars in stylistics and curriculum for English department TAs
- The design and building of specially equipped composition classrooms ready for television and computer work
- Special workshops for several professional schools
- Three different kinds of adjunct courses attached to courses in other departments

Because the last-named on this list—the adjunct courses—play so large a part in our campus strategy, they deserve fuller description. I knew we were going to be under pressure to create an upper division or exit proficiency exam in composition. This seemed to me the wrong pedagogy, expensive and pointless. The real solution was to make sure that writing was assigned and read in upper-division courses. A proficiency exam is bound to seem a negative and irrelevant barrier to the students who pass it; to those who fail, the remedial course is bound to seem punitive. If we were to avoid the Kitzhaber effect* we would have to put the writing where it ought to be anyway, in courses. There were two ways to spread writing "across the curriculum," as such teaching is now described. You could try, through blandishment and moral exhortation, to make your colleagues assign and correct more writing, teaching them how to do this if necessary. This is how most programs of this sort have proceeded. Or you could supply this kind of teaching as a free service to those instructors who wanted it. We chose the second way. A faculty so large, heterogeneous, busy, and research-oriented as UCLA's seemed to be very unlikely to change their teaching patterns much just because one English professor became the campus scold and got after them. On the other hand, many professors were very much in favor of assigning more writing but, faced with a class of five hundred, hardly knew how to do it. We tried three models of adjunct instruction in 1979–80, to see which one would best suit these UCLA circumstances. A memo written at the time describes them:

Adjunct: An English 3 [English 3 was the basic freshman composition course] *attached to a large lecture course in another department.*

The English 3 adjunct course satisfies the composition requirement. Students must be concurrently enrolled in the base course—and in any labs or discussion sections that course requires. It meets three times a week, in one-hour sessions, for four units of credit. English department TAs teach sections of 25 students each.

Like other English 3s, this course offers basic and thorough training in exposition and argument; students write and revise essays, analyze prose passages, and review, as necessary, grammar and mechanics.

---

* Albert R. Kitzhaber, *Themes, Theories, and Therapy* (New York, 1963). Kitzhaber studied the writing program at Dartmouth College and found that though improvement came in the freshman year, if students didn't continue to write, by senior year they were right back where they had started as freshmen.

Unlike other English 3s, it selects reading and writing assignments from the base course materials. Instructors meet with a TA from the other department, a consultant who provides sample essay and exam topics and discusses base course standards and requirements.

Intensive: A 2-unit writing-intensive course attached to a course in another department. Recommended for upper division courses.

The writing-intensive course does not fulfill a composition requirement: it exists solely as a writing supplement to the base course. It offers two units of credit toward graduation, though not toward a major. It meets once a week for two hours with an English instructor.

Component: A writing component included in another department's course.

The writing component exists only within the structure of the course to which it is added. It fulfills no composition requirement and offers no additional credit.

A writing consultant from the English department conducts a writing workshop, evaluates one set of papers, holds student conferences, and returns for a follow-up workshop. The workshops require three hours of class time: conferences may be held during or after class.

The Intensives and Components worked well and have been greatly expanded. The adjunct sections of English 3 proved too hard to schedule and were dropped. Obviously, at the beginning the absolute numbers of the Intensives would be small. But as UCLA moved closer to an upper-division writing requirement, as we thought it would, we could expand their scope. The machinery would all be in place and attached to just the kind of inquiry the student had selected as an area of special interest.

Such an expansion would, of course, be very expensive. And even then it could hardly provide the continual practice in writing and revising for all undergraduates that we would like to see. Here we came up against the same seemingly hopeless blank wall that writing instruction faces at any level. The teaching of writing is surely the most labor-intensive activity on earth. It ranks right up there with scrimshaw and knitting with a no. 0 needle. It requires talented, trained, and energetic teachers, and yet when you teach it for a long time uninterrupted, it softens your brain. And the burned-out teacher is as much a long-range problem as the labor-intensiveness of the activity. I could see only one way out of this impasse—electronic repetition. Replacing the teacher by the machine seemed to me out of the question. People write for people. Computers were not going to be able to grade student writings or discuss the structure of ideas which a student was trying to dredge from the depths of vague understanding. The great simplicity of the first-wave CAI dream— no teachers, just banks of screens—wasn't going to work for writing any more than it did for any kind of intuitive learning. But much student writing error is repetitive. If some of that could be drained off to electronic instruction, the teacher would be less bored and instruction less expensive. Here, as elsewhere, the economics would be economics of scale. We would have to plan from the start for a campus-wide program. A market of sixty thousand seemed from this perspective an advantage. And if we could come up with successful products—TV programs or computer programs—the potential market was much, much bigger—the whole of American higher education. This vision of sugarplums could justify a lot of start-up expense: we could consider experimental teaching as product-development. From it might come a series of television-computer-text modules that would, over twenty years, say, amortize the whole program.

So much for dreaming. To put it into practice, I started at home. I had just published a little textbook called *Revising Prose.* It was built on a simple thesis: student writing these days was trying to be bu-reaucratic writing, trying to mimic what I called "The Official Style." It did this in some easy, machine-readable ways: too many prepositional phrases, too many "to be" verbs, too many Latinate "tion" or "sion" words, too many long sentences, etc. I knew a computer could diagnose these problems, because two students of mine had proved it by writing a program which did just that. I hired them to develop the program and begin to use it, if we could get some instructors interested, in regular classes.

Now we needed a television program. The history here was a little deeper. I had for a long time thought that the basic kind of prose analysis involved in stylistic revision would really be better taught on a CRT display than in a codex book. I tried word-processors, but they could not do sufficiently complex manipulations. Finally, through the help of the Office of Instructional Development (OID) at UCLA (which has as a central responsibility the use of media in instruction), I was introduced to a character-generator, the machine used to make titles and special effects for television news programs. The machine UCLA used was named CHYRON, and I was heartened by the classical precedent. It could do all that I wanted it to in the way of animated print display, and in sixty-four colors. It had been bought to title a series of medical films, but the vice-chancellor in charge of OID immediately sensed what I was trying to do with it; if I could come up with a script in two weeks, she would make a thirty-minute cassette by the end of the summer (we were then in June of 1979). I did and she did. We thought the pilot looked pretty good and started trying it out. It was not a talking-heads, classroom-in-action kind of production at all. Just dynamic graphics and animated print displays that illustrated the procedures of *Revising Prose*.

We now had one module, at least in pilot form: a finished book, a computer program, and a television cassette. The book would be tried out in the marketplace; we would try out the media accompaniments at UCLA, and elsewhere if occasion served. I had no idea at this point—autumn of 1979—that it would take the best part of two years to debug the procedure and get a marketable product and plan a coherent UCLA delivery system. The book began to sell and has continued to. No problems there. Its "paramedic method" seemed to work. We began showing the TV pilot everywhere we could find an audience: at all levels of instruction at UCLA, from jocks to check-book-wielding administrators, to outside groups that ranged from the Santa Barbara District Attorney's Office to the Congressional Budget Office in Washington. It worked. The CHYRON machine was able to bring eye and ear together in a dynamic way much better suited to prose analysis than a codex book. We needed several revisions and three narrations to get it right, but the machine itself seemed clearly a promising format. The computer program went through several revisions and expansions. It worked too, though it depended more than the TV program on being properly placed in a controlled pedagogical sequence.

The Delivery System. While these experiments were going forward, it was necessary to design a delivery system for them at UCLA. From the beginning it seemed to me that such a system would, in broad outline at least, be highly generalizable to most university campuses. If our development costs could not be recouped just at UCLA, they would certainly be amortizable if spread over the whole system of higher education in California—all the university and state university campuses. And they would work elsewhere just as well. What would a delivery system look like?

Our campus survey had revealed at least four basic professional languages at UCLA: the official styles of social science, natural science, and administration, and the more traditional academic essay style of the humanities. Clearly we would need pedagogies tailored to each of these areas. They could cover elementary instruction for students who planned to work in these areas as well as instruction for students already at work there. We would need a three-tiered program: a general beginning module; second-tier modules for the basic professional language areas; and third-tier modules for particular large courses. The student would follow a progression like this: (1) Basic instruction in the beginning writing courses. The student would view the television program as part of classroom instruction, then write a paper, submit it to the computer for editing, then, when the computer released it, submit it to the instructor. (2) After selecting a major, the student would watch the applicable second-tier TV program and, as papers were assigned (increasingly, in Writing Intensive sections), he would submit them to the computer for detailed editing tailored to his field of concentration. (3) Then, for the basic (and at UCLA very large) courses, he would have a TV program aimed at the work to be done in that class. Again, TV program, writing of paper, computer editing, submission. This ought to confront the instructor with a paper far more carefully and self-consciously revised than before. The computer diagnosis, though very simple, could flag the kinds of stylistic qualities that obscured the student's thinking, both for the student and for the instructor. Clear out this sludge and both could concentrate on the basic problems in argumentation and evidence.

Such, at least, were the intended joys. On their basis, I drew up the following ambitious plan in the autumn term of 1979. I quote from a memo:

  A. The *Revising Prose* Programs and Packages
    1. First-Level TV Tapes
      a. The Basic Package for UCLA students (undergraduate and graduate)
        (1) *Revising Prose*
        (2) *Revising Prose* TV program
        (3) *Revising Prose* computer program
        (4) *Revising Prose* Exercises TV program
      b. The Basic Package for Law, Business, and Administration
        (1) *Revising Bureaucratic Prose*
        (2) *Revising Bureaucratic Prose* TV program
        (3) *Revising Bureaucratic Prose* computer program
        (4) *Revising Bureaucratic Prose* Exercises TV program
    2. Second-Level TV Tapes
      a. The Freshman English paper
      b. The Undergraduate paper in the Social Sciences
      c. The Undergraduate paper in the Humanities
      d. The Undergraduate paper/lab report in the Physical Sciences
      e. Professional Writing in the Social Sciences
      f. Professional Writing in the Humanities
      g. Professional Writing in the Physical Sciences
    3. Third-Level TV Tapes
      a. The Undergraduate paper in English (etc. for each large department)
      b. The Graduate paper in English (etc. for each large department)
        (1) Legal Prose
        (2) Business Prose
        (3) Administrative Prose
        (4) Medical Prose
        (5) Accounting Prose (etc. for each major field)

Such a triple-tiered plan would, when completed, serve as the basis of further planning. And the various nonstudent campus constituencies could use these same materials, since they belonged to the same professional language-groups.

How did it work out in the real world? Not nearly so fast as I had hoped. As I write this in the autumn of 1982, we have a final first-level *Revising Prose* module—text, computer program, TV cassette. We have one published special field text—*Revising Business Prose*—and a TV script for it ready for production. We have one award-winning TV cassette on medical writing written by a staff member. We have a lot of material accumulated and a lot of experience. Why not a faster progress?

Homo proponit. Deus disponit. First of all, we didn't begin to have the money required. And we encountered smaller vexations in spending the money we did have. The television studio shut down for six months' remodeling. The campus open-access instructional computer—an ancient DEC 10—died of old age. The administration could not agree on a replacement. The PLATO system we tried seemed not to fit our plans or budget. And I couldn't find people to do the TV scripts for us. I was surprised, in fact, by a kind of Luddite resistance to the whole idea of electronic intermediation. I now no longer question the research of Lewis Solomon of UCLA on the difficulties of retraining humanists. They are, he has found, likely to be not only the most narrowly educated group on campus but the most inelastic and unadaptable as well. We began to experience this unadaptability, and it slowed us down. Our administrative and financial arrangements were all wrong, too. I had thought we could run the series like a learned journal. We have had to reorganize it into something far more like a TV production company. And so on through a series of genuine "learning experiences." Meanwhile, the pilot module we have been able to put in place works wonderfully well. The computer diagnosis makes the student self-conscious about his predictable bad habits. The TV cassette is being shown four times a day across campus. The premises and plans still look good. It remains to find the money that will get the power to the rear wheels.

Part of the delivery system had to be some redesigned classrooms. Again with the support of the Office of Instructional Development, we removed the screwed-to-the-floor, forward-facing seats in two classrooms used for composition and redecorated them with carpeting, drapes, comfortable swivel chairs on casters, and movable tables. I wanted from the beginning to allow the instructors to put before the students more text, revised and unrevised, than a chalkboard could easily allow. We tried white magic-marker boards instead, serving as boards and projector screens, with overhead and opaque projectors in each room and electric typewriters in place to generate copy for the projector. I wanted to see if we couldn't get more text in front of the students during revision exercises. None of these projection tricks worked. The instructors, with a few exceptions, didn't want to bother rethinking the problem in new terms. The redecorating, however, proved a great success. That the two really liveable, attractive classrooms in the English building were devoted to composition instruction was an eloquent allegory of what we were trying to do for composition teaching at UCLA.

We tried something more ambitious for a third room, a total redesign for television projection, with built-in monitors the students could see without breaking eye-contact with their fellow students. The whole show was controllable from the instructor's position. Again, no new pedagogy or thought from the by-their-nature-imaginative-and-adaptable humanists. It will work when we get a full range of TV modules, but my hope that doing it a little early might stimulate new teaching ideas got nowhere.

Our other great failure was an attempt to create a rhetoric concentration as part of the Ph.D. in English. This, for various reasons, came to nought. In other graduate and professional fields we did a bit better: for the law school a one-week late-summer seminar for the legal drafting faculty; a pilot program for the Graduate School of Management; some pioneering work in the medical school, and so on. We did generate a lot of teaching for a cadre staff, but it was testing, not a full-scale program. That was to come in 1980–81.

Amidst these labors, we spent the spring of 1980 in two other large endeavors. We planned and established a semiautonomous subsection of the English department, called the Composition Section. And we mounted a seven-week national recruitment program and hired thirty-two people to staff both the Composition Section and the Writing Programs. Since both these undertakings presented problems that seem to be of general interest and prompt repeated questioning, it may be worthwhile to treat them in a little detail.

The Composition Section. Large state universities like UCLA, once they decide that the literacy crisis is going to be around for some time, must decide how to convert the varied ad hoc answers to the problem which have grown up informally, into a centrally directed administrative unit. (They can, of course, decide simply to let things go on as they have been. It's a choice but not one that will last for long. Some kind of central direction is essential.) The central unit can be one of three kinds: (1) entirely within the English department; (2) a new department; (3) a composite unit somewhere between the two. The first and second choices make for a much more symmetrical administrative chain of command, a department being really the only integer a university structure can handle with any grace or polish. To put everything in the English department is to put it where this kind of instruction has traditionally lived and where everyone expects it to be. To put it into a separate department requires a readjustment in faculty expectation, but after that the accepted departmental structure takes over and people know who you are. All the rules fit you, and you take your place in the great democracy of academic departments. We chose neither of these obviously attractive patterns. Why?

The first choice would have blurred and distended the department's professional focus. The second would have taken instruction in composition further from the English department than we wanted it to go. The department recognized the importance of composition instruction. They realized, though, that it was growing into something very different from what a university-level English department was trained and accustomed to do, and was bound to become more different yet. We would try to remain under the departmental roof for courses which had traditionally been offered by the department—that would be the Composition Section—but also to preserve the UCLA Writing Programs as the experimental wing of the enterprise. The Composition Section would report through the letters and science deans. Here we had a model. The English department had a dozen years ago spun off a subsection for English-as-a-Second-Language instruction. The Composition Section would function as the ESL Section did, reporting to the deans. After twenty-some hours of meetings we agreed on a written proposal which I had drafted and which the English department approved. I would be the vice-chairman of the department for composition and would be responsible for instruction in all the composition courses offered by the department. But we could appoint instructors only with approval of the department executive committee and were to be overseen by an advisory committee upon which the English chairman and the appropriate dean were to sit, ex officio. It promised a flexible combination of independent action and traditional academic authority, and so it has proved. We have been able to remain close to the English department and yet, through the Writing Programs, move swiftly in a number of areas where well-bred English departments rightly fear to tread.

Recruitment and Hiring. It remained to staff both programs in time for the following autumn. We faced, actually, two kinds of staffing problems. We needed to have a dozen people with special training of one kind or another for the various special courses offered in the Writing Programs. We also needed at least twenty people to staff the regular freshman courses. As with many large university English departments, our graduate enrollments had fallen precipitously—50 percent in three years. This meant fewer TAs in the future, a shortage likely to endure. At the same time, our undergraduate major was thriving and no regular ladder-track faculty could be spared from the literature offerings to teach the composition courses. How were these to be staffed?

Not by regular tenure-track appointments. Both the English department and the administration felt that too little was known about the literacy crisis or how long it would last to build a permanent organization. We would have to hire under the Visiting Lecturer category, a one-year appointment renewable for up to a maximum of four years. I saw only one way to make such an appointment both fair and attractive. We would have to pay well, keep the teaching load low, and try to provide something like a post-doctoral training and research program in composition. We could, then, offer our lecturers a chance to teach and write in several areas of the literacy crisis, and this would render them more employable than a traditional English Ph.D., either in the private sector or in the academy. The salary and teaching load of the Visiting Lecturer were already competitive, and we would try to distribute the teaching load over the many kinds of courses we offer. We would begin a staff seminar which met every two weeks to discuss major research issues or texts in composition. We would offer training in computer use, word processing, the use of overhead projectors, and so on. We would try to offer the collegial atmosphere so often lacking in composition programs, with their hordes of part-timers checking in for three nights a week.

We managed, after a hectic hiring campaign in which the six of us who staffed the Writing Programs the first year read over 350 applications and interviewed ninety people in Los Angeles and across the country, to hire the thirty-plus people we needed. They came, and because they were such a splendid group of people, we were able to create the collegial atmosphere we had hoped for and in the way we had planned. We held a full week of orientation lectures and meetings, and after that people found their way around campus with a minimum of confusion. We were able, happily, to renew almost all the appointments for a second year in the autumn of the first, so that they did not have yet another year of job-seeking to live through. Some of the people we hired had finished the degree and had been teaching; others were still writing dissertations; a few were especially trained in composition; all the rest had wide teaching experience in the field. We were impressed by published research but were looking first for bright and energetic teachers.

Planning Strategies

Three main lessons have emerged from our efforts so far: the need for a campus-wide strategy in writing instruction; the need for a regional strategy which locates you in the educational sequence of which you are a part; and the need to think carefully about the long-term relationship of composition instruction to the rest of the curriculum in which it exists.

A carefully administered campus-wide strategy seems to me, at least for institutions as large as UCLA, both the most efficient and the most adaptable kind of organization. The literacy crisis has been caused by a failure of educational sequence which has now cycled through the whole educational chain, from kindergarten through graduate school. The organization which aims to deal with it must be able to look at the whole sequence. I began with this view as basic administrative premise. If we kept on with a dozen vaguely related tutorial agencies, projects, and regular courses, we would never get anywhere. But as we began to survey the campus and bring its writing problems into a coherent form, other advantages of a central office began to emerge. Hiring, for one. Many parts of the campus knew they had a writing problem but did not know how to diagnose it or hire the right people to remedy it. A central office could do this and give the people it hired a professional focus and collegiality they could never have if they were hired singly and scattered across the campus. We also found that size brought adaptability. Because we had a fluid body of manpower we could move swiftly into new areas, make teaching readjustments on a campus-wide basis. If one thing didn't work we could try another—right now. We could begin to think in a genuinely sequential way, try to construct possible educational progressions that different types of students might want to follow. We could end the curricular and pedagogical isolation in which teachers were foundering across campus. And we could plan and operate on a scale that made media programs possible, for only on a large scale would they be worth the investment.

But more than any of these, the campus-wide survey and perspective allowed us to diagnose the problem in a new way. We had to confront the several professional languages written on campus and decide how to teach—or to revise—them. We came up against the enormous English-as-a-Second Language problem at UCLA and began to put it in the frame of long-term campus planning. We were able, in these ways and many more, to think about how the literacy crisis would affect the campus as a whole and what long-range planning seemed required to meet it.

Beyond a campus-wide strategy looms the equally important regional one. The literacy problem stretches as far as the educational sequence of which your institution forms a part. These sequences vary widely from region to region but for the most part do remain regional. The genuinely national university campuses form a still small minority, and even they have sequences, though rarely defined ones. UCLA has a clearly defined one. Half of its undergraduates come from the Los Angeles Unified School District and over two-thirds of them from

Southern California. Southern California's problems are going to be UCLA's problems just as sure as children grow up. We will teach some of these students and teach the teachers of a great many more. Let me quote parts of yet another memo, in which I tried to put UCLA in its regional context:

> *Failure of Sequence and Demographic Change.* We began by assuming that the literacy crisis was caused, in large part, by a massive failure of educational sequence from kindergarten through senior high. For the teaching of literacy, and literature, the whole sequence would have to be rebuilt. Or, rather, built anew, since the old curriculum and training were manifestly unsuited to present circumstances. From the beginning the problem seemed at least a generation long. It was not a short-term oscillation of educational fashion but a genuine long-term emergency.

The demographic changes that the memo describes next have already been discussed on pages 107 and 115–17 above, along with the increasing multilingual strain on the public school system. To look further ahead:

> A chronic shortage of public money promises to make all this worse. The schools will get less money to cope with the language crisis even as a society short of needed social services will create yet more social problems for the schools. It all makes for a vicious downward spiral that will intensify middle-class flight from the schools and further demoralize the now-majority minorities. . . .
>
> *The Linguistic Time Bomb.* America has an enormous tradition of, and urge to, monolingualism. That tradition won't evaporate. But the pressure toward multilingualism is broad-scaled and intense. That pressure won't go away either, and together the two forces could cause a social explosion. The monolingual tradition will endure in middle-class America and in the Establishment, but the non-English-speaking classes, led on by 50 years of rising expectations, will find it increasingly hard to learn the language that opens the Establishment door. For the first time in our history, class differences will be isomorphic with intrenched language differences. Whatever the social outcome of this linguistic class structure (and a look at Quebec or Belgium doesn't reassure one much), the effect on English-language instruction will be electric. *Every* issue becomes politically charged in a way that will make the current bilingualism debate

look like a Buckingham Palace garden party. The obverse of this danger, of course, implies that English composition instruction becomes, not an embarrassed fuss over our verbal ps and qs, but a major political concern. If the time bomb is defused, language instruction will play a large part in the defusing.

Everything we think and all we do should take its bearings from this kind of regional assessment. Ambitious state universities have for the last thirty years measured their sophistication by their national perspective, their distance from local problems. The national perspective which fits individual disciplines, at least sometimes, often does not fit a campus as a whole, and especially not its undergraduate curriculum. For planning a writing curriculum, the national perspective may be a disaster. You must look at the educational chain of being where you actually find yourself and look to what your place is, and ought to be, in it. A campus-wide perspective forces you to do this.

These two new perspectives, the campus view and the regional view, suggest how an ambitious writing program might fit into the campus curriculum. We can begin with the word *remediation*. Most of the discussion about the kind of work done in the Writing Programs focuses on remediation. Yet, with a massive failure of educational sequence such as we now face, in a sense *all* education becomes remedial, falls below its proper level. The biggest writing problems our campus survey unearthed were those faced by Ph.D. students trying to write a dissertation. At the same time, paradoxically, all the work of the Writing Programs might just as well be viewed as *honors* work. It tries to *intensify* the student's experience, in whatever field, clarify and focus a student's thought, lead him to a level of work the system does not normally demand. Isn't this the honors impulse?

Clearly, we need a better word than *remediation*. The campus-wide writing program aims at improving the quality of the student's entire education. It is a great mistake to think that in every case we can hope only to regain a former level of quality. For instance, I might cite an Intensive that we attached to a chemistry course in which the students write up a long research report. The Intensive instructors knew no chemistry, and they spent a great deal of time in trying to cope with the difficulties this raised. But the difficulty turned out to be an advantage for the students, who learned more chemistry, they said, because they had to explain what they were doing to the Intensive instructors. The instructors, in their turn, learned a lot about the need for a professional language and about how that particular one works. The professor who taught the course remarked that the issues brought up by the Intensives had improved the critical thinking done in the whole course. What resulted was not remediation at all, but several steps in the direction of informal honors.

No one could give our tentative steps into computer-assisted instruction more than a C+, but even there the campus-wide perspective suggested a new direction, based on the computer's potential use as a focus for interdisciplinary instruction. That our students need to learn something about computers seems beyond argument. They will live in a computer-based world. That English composition should take a special interest in computer literacy seems equally beyond question. Words are increasingly being composed and transmitted electronically, from CRT display to CRT display, not by words inscribed on a piece of paper. No one knows how this will change reading and writing—this is one of the many exciting areas of composition research opening up—but it will clearly affect them strongly. Our students must at least know the moves of this new game before they take their place in business and government. They must know what word-processing is, how computer-based editing and typesetting techniques work, what the electronic intermediation of words is all about.

But computer literacy should mean more than this. It should explore the social and philosophical implications of the computer revolution, not simply introduce students to elementary number-crunching. The history of information storage and retrieval in Western civilization did not begin with the Univac. It began with poetic formulae in the poems of Homer. And it has remained for much of its history a literary phenomenon. The debate over a computer's "artificial intelligence" and man's intuitive brain begins not with the AI labs at MIT but with Plato's case against the rhetoricians, an encounter that surfaces again in modern phenomenological thinking, as Hubert Dreyfus shows in his brilliant *What Computers Can't Do.*

A computer literacy course, then, should not be just a bag of electronic disks and a new vocabulary. It should have some intellectual depth. To contrast how human intelligence and computer intelligence work takes us into a dozen disciplines, but nowhere do the opportunities shine more brightly than in language. The synergistic context of human language and computer language could galvanize the freshman course in writing.

All these programs and plans add up to a new kind of activity, and one that is destined to endure, at least in the large public land-grant university. The first social task of the large public university was to aid and abet a society basically agricultural. It did this through the Agricultural School, of course, but also through a curriculum and extracurriculum—and a school calendar—suited to an agricultural society. With the coming of industrialization the state university subtly realigned itself to serve a new kind of economy—a goods economy. To this period belongs not only the rise of pure science but the creation of the engineering schools and technical institutions which the pure scientists so often deplored and opposed. The service economy brought another series of changes. At the center of them, it can be argued, stood the rise of the social sciences. Now we stand on the verge of another basic change, a realignment to serve an information economy, a technological culture that depends on verbal and mathematical symbols as never before. This economy is going to demand a new kind of study, one that has emerged here and there recently but has never really been properly named. We might call it "Humanist Engineering." It will stand to English, say, or history, as the Engineering school stands to physics or chemistry. It will concentrate not only on acquiring new knowledge but on the delivery systems needed to socialize that knowledge. It will stand, as engineering schools do now, with one foot on campus and the other in the world.

This kind of structure, new to the American campus, will not be new to Western education. It is exactly what the Greek rhetoricians had in mind when they talked about *paideia*. And that Greek tradition, at a far-distanced remove, constitutes both English composition's ancestor and its logical fulfillment and intellectual home.

A New Humanist Curriculum

Perhaps we can now see how the Writing Programs' efforts, practical and locally shaped as they have been, bear upon the humanist curriculum with which I began this chapter. If remediation represents the least ambitious—though not the least important—part of what we do, surely the desire to place composition in a larger humanist curriculum represents the most ambitious. Yet if it is to work, it cannot emerge from an ideological presentation of the case, or indeed from any direct presentation of the case at all. It must come, as I argued at the beginning of this chapter, from an effort to meet and serve people where they are. It must come, that is to say, from trying to solve the literacy crisis in every way one can think of.

I think this is beginning to happen. For example, I argued several years ago in *Style: An Anti-Textbook* (1974) that the only natural subject of the course in composition is style itself, and that it is stylistic self-consciousness—the *At* vision, in terms of my earlier metaphor—which reveals to us the ornamental side of human nature, the side emerging as game and play. We did not diagnose the writing problem at UCLA in terms of this thesis at all, but the diagnosis nevertheless seemed to realize this thesis in action. For stylistic self-consciousness emerges by the very nature of the case from the campus-wide and regional strategies. If you face, as the basis of your thinking, several different professional styles on campus and a multilingual society off campus and increasingly on campus as well, the *At/Through* oscillation will be triggered simply by your day-to-day efforts to cope with the problem. It helps enormously to have a theoretical framework in which to place these day-to-day efforts, but you are not imposing the framework on the problem. The force flows the other way.

In such a polyglot case, you inevitably find yourself trying to invent and preserve a common language. This will be English, thinking in the multilingual social context: it will be a kind of English agile and spacious enough to contain all the professional languages and yet able to speak to all, thus nonprofessional whenever and wherever it can be. Amid the alarms and excursions of daily teaching it is not easy to see, but we are trying to reinvent a Drydenian middle style, one to replace the Official Style which threatens to anesthetize our sociality. It is interesting in this connection to reflect on what we have learned from the Writing Intensive experience. We started out thinking that though we were adding this service from outside a course, ideally it ought to come from within, from the main course and the main instructor. The adjunct type of course was only a temporary expedient. Now I am not so sure. What the Intensive instructor brings to the course is an *At* vision that complements the *Through* vision of the main instructor. The course is arranged under the assumption that style and content are separable, with an instructor for each. This, again, was not a theoretical assumption; it simply came along with the problem as the only feasible way to solve it. When the Intensives really work, however, the students—and often the instructors!—find that style and content are not separable. That is, they set in motion precisely the *At/Through* oscillation I have been talking about throughout these essays. It may be that the "outside observer," the "visiting anthropologist for composition," brings to the course a perspective which can be added in no other way.

And over the long run it will work in the other direction, too. Teaching in the Intensives will give the writing instructors an idea of what is happening across a broad range of disciplines. Equipped with this multidisciplinary sophistication, they can then begin to understand the core curriculum. The curriculum built on a common theory of motive which I began this chapter by describing emerges naturally from composition teaching. Thus we may be redeemed by the problem, *equipped* to deal with it by *trying* to deal with it. And we shall find the same logic operating in other areas as well. If we try to give our students the education they need in the computer, or more largely the electronic, processing of words, we shall see how the basic distinction between electronic numerical and human intuitive mentation really works itself out in a number of disciplines. That will show us how it should be built into a freshman course in computer literacy.

The traditional "humanities" course has been built on a syllabus of texts that represented, when it first came together, all that seemed worth knowing. We need now to institute the Renaissance example again, but we cannot do so if we don't know what is known, at least in outline, and what new ways of knowing have been developed to know it. We are told that knowledge is too complex, that no one can know it all. Well, no one can be a genuine Leonardo-style polymath, but as far as the broad outlines and general conclusions, of course we can know them. What else can a liberal education be about? Our efforts to cope with the literacy crisis on a campus-wide basis put us in the way of acquiring just this knowledge in the course of doing our regular work. When there were old-fashioned humanities courses, it used to be often said that you got your liberal education by being assigned as a young professor to teach them. It was true then, and it is going to be true now for the new kind of humanistic course. Such a course is emerging in a different way, but what would we expect? It is going to be a very different kind of course.

And might it not profit, as those who teach it certainly will, from what goes on in the graduate and especially in the professional schools? After all, it is for advanced inquiry of these kinds that the core curriculum must provide the foundation. I think, in fact, that we can generalize the point. The kind of teaching offered by a campus-wide composition plan restores to all who do it a sense of American education as a sequence. If you teach high-school and elementary-school teachers, or if you teach remedial basic skills courses at the university level, you learn that college students *come from somewhere,* that they have a past. If you teach a legal writing seminar, or a workshop in pulmonary medicine, you learn something about where they will go after the undergraduate years. You get some idea of education *as a sequence;* you also may begin to think about what an *orderly* sequence might look like. The terrible compartmentalization of American academic life begins to break down. This alone confers a tremendous advantage.

When the first humanist revival came to Europe in the Renaissance, it came as a result not only of a scholarly revolution—the rediscovery of classical texts—but also from a crisis of public literacy as hydra-headed as our own, one that comprehended the unsettling dangers of a Bible in English, the decay of church education following the Reformation, and an unprecedented social need for effective vernacular communication that would serve a plethora of new social, political, and economic purposes. These forces came together with a particular incandescence because they were at the same time worldly and schol-arly, responding to immediate social needs and exquisitely centered in a study of the word, a study of style. Is our current state so different? We have, in modern semiotics and stylistics, an academic concentration on the word of awesome power and penetration. We have, heaven knows, a crisis in public literacy of epidemic proportions. Our problem is to bring them together. Our mixture of the two will be our "humanism"; that is why literary study and composition instruction must not be allowed to drift off into separate, hermetically— and perhaps hermeneutically—sealed compartments.

One thing we can be sure of. If a new definition of the "humanities" and the humanities curriculum really is lurking in the wings, then the campus-wide address to the writing problem will, over a dozen years, discover it and bring it into focus. We do not need to force the issue and should not. If the consensus is there, it will emerge. But it needs an agency to emerge through, a stage to be born on. That, I think, is where the campus-wide composition program comes in. We will have in mind a theory of the curriculum sufficiently deep and capacious to tell us what kind of curriculum is waiting to be born, wants to be created. We will not have to impose it from above. We will have seen it emerge from our attempts to solve a real and pressing social problem. We will, in real truth, have been present at the creation of a genuinely new humanism.

That, at least, is what I hope will be the next chapter at UCLA.

Index

About the Author

Richard A. Lanham is professor of English and executive director of the UCLA Writing Programs at the University of California, Los Angeles.

His books include: *Sidney's Old Arcadia* (1965); *A Handlist of Rhetorical Terms* (1968); *"Tristram Shandy": The Games of Pleasure* (1973); *Style: An Anti-Textbook* (1974); *The Motives of Eloquence: Literary Rhetoric in the Renaissance* (1976); *Revising Prose* (1979); *Revising Business Prose* (1981); *Analyzing Prose* (1983); and *Literacy and the Survival of Humanism* (1983).